MARANATHA

MARANATHA

*Reflections on the Mystical Theology
of John the Evangelist*

by
William J. Fulco, S.J.

PAULIST PRESS
New York / Paramus / Toronto

Library of Congress
Catalog Card Number: 73-82225

ISBN: 0-8091-1778-9

Published by Paulist Press
Editorial Office: 1865 Broadway, N.Y., N.Y. 10023
Business Office: 400 Sette Drive, Paramus, N.J. 07652

Printed and bound in the
United States of America

Contents

Preface

Although I have had to grapple with them in my own research into the Johannine writings of the New Testament, it is not my purpose in this book to pursue and suggest answers for literary, source-critical or historical problems. I am concerned solely with certain aspects of John's world-view, his experience of God, and his teachings on the Christian enterprise, insofar as these may enlighten our own spiritual pilgrimage and move us toward a fuller share in the Life that Jesus came to give us more abundantly. These facets of his thought shine out in his writings regardless of what stance the scholar may take toward a host of other matters.

I presuppose the basic literary unity of the Gospel of John and the three letters of the New Testament attributed to him. In both cases I admit the strong probability of various layers of redaction, but see a special value in studying these documents in the final form in which the Church accepted them as accurately and richly expressing herself and her experience to the faithful.

In attempting to understand the evolution of John's thought, I consider that the First Letter was written before the Gospel, at least before the final written form of the Gospel. In general there is a movement from vagueness to clarity between the Letter and the Gospel, and almost invariably the precisions of the Gospel are in a direct developmental line of thought from statements in the Letter. This is particularly noticeable in passages with references to eschatology, to the role of the Spirit, to the relationship between the Father and Jesus, and, in general, in the employment of certain key Johannine words.

Although most critics would not admit the direct Johannine authorship of the Apocalypse for a variety of good reasons, most scholars would place this writing within the Johannine school of theology. For this reason I occasionally make use of it where I think it appropriate.

Translations both of Old Testament and New Testament passages are my own.

I am very grateful to the several people who have particularly encouraged me to put my reflections on St. John in writing, most especially Fathers Jack Boyle, S.J. and John Wright, S.J., both of whom offered me many helpful criticisms and suggestions. Three friends and former students of mine were a special stimulus by sharing with me their own insights into and enthusiasm for John: Fathers Terrance Sweeney, S.J., Michael Moynahan, S.J., and Thomas Rausch, S.J.

I dedicate this book to Tom with gratitude and affection.

Berkeley, California
November 1972

Foreword

The difficulties in approaching the Johannine writings of the New Testament as a basis for a coherent and comprehensible personal Christian spirituality are considerable. Some of the problems are rooted in a certain mystique which surrounds Johannine studies. Classical introductions to John bristle with references to gnosticism, the Mandaeans, Qumran, Greek philosophy and, of course, Rudolph Bultmann. The average layman becomes convinced that John's spiritual vision is inaccessible to him without a vast background of technical scholarship.

Most authors dealing with Christian spirituality and mysticism within the context of the New Testament seem to lean very heavily on Paul's writings, and, except for passing references, relegate John to the more esoteric pursuits of criticism and dogmatic theology. The fact that John is so quotable has not helped either. "God is love" and "I am the Way, the Truth and the Life" can be repeated so often and so emptily that they lose their meaning, richness and necessary context.

There are, of course, problems intrinsic to the nature, style, vocabulary and perspective of John's writings themselves. For one thing, John's "logic" and development are not linear. He does not move from proposition to proposition, not even from insight to insight. His style, rather, is cyclic, continually returning in waves to the same themes (all of which are present at least implicitly even in the Prologue of the Gospel), each time from a deeper or different perspective. This means that one cannot comfortably assimilate a later statement of the Johannine vision until he has made his own the depths that came earlier. Each fragment of his mosaic takes on definition only in the evolving context of each other fragment.

What is more, because we have in the past placed too much emphasis on the "Greek" aspects of the Johannine corpus, we are too ready to view his key ideas such as *life* and *truth* as quite abstract, forgetting that John's background is decidedly Hebraic and "existential." *Life* and *truth, love* and *light*—these all have meanings which we can verify or at least look for in our own experience. They are concepts very germane to our everyday world of living, suffering, rejoicing, in our inner and interpersonal universe of seeking to understand ourselves, our efforts to love one another, and our quest to find meaning and purpose in our lives.

Once the basic vocabulary and perspective of John's Gospel and letters are grasped, prayer is probably a better tool for understanding John than reading a wealth of commentaries.

Maranatha, the title of this book, is a liturgical exclamation of the early Church. It is found at the end of Paul's First Letter to the Corinthians (16:22) and in the *Didache* (10:6). It is an Aramaic expression, "Our Lord, come!" It occurs in a translated form at the close of the Apocalypse, in the last lines of the entire Bible. Jesus proclaims, "Yes! I am coming soon!" The Christian, whose hope awaits Jesus' coming as his salvation and the consummation of his history, sums up and confesses his entire faith in one spirited response, "Amen! Come, Lord Jesus!" (Apoc 22:20)

1. My Spirit Thirsts

I thirst for God, for the living God;
when shall I go and behold the face of God? (Ps 42:2)

Pervading every level of the Old Testament is an obsession with finding access to and union with God. When Israel is at prayer, this is its constant theme: "O God, you are my God, I long for you. My spirit thirsts for you, my flesh pines for you." (Ps 63:1) "For God alone do I wait in silence." (Ps 62:1)

The desire for communion with God seems, for example, to have been the common element in all of the varied sacrifices offered in Israel's cult, whether a sacrifice was intended to remove obstacles to such a union, as with atonement sacrifices, or whether it was to celebrate fellowship with God, as in peace offerings.

Law, too, was thought of as revealing the parameters of God's operation in Israel's history. If the people were to experience Yahweh's saving presence among them, the law was to spell out for them the limits beyond which there could be no encounter with him.

Even in late Old Testament times when the cult was moribund and when the conviction grew that Yahweh's saving acts were either a remembrance of the past or a hope of the future, the underlying rationale of the good and prosperous life as described in the occasionally cynical maxims of Israel's sages seems to be that prosperity bespeaks a harmony with the inner laws of the uni-

5

verse, and indicates thereby at least an oblique union
with God, who governs the universe with his wisdom.

Yahweh is salvation. In him is deliverance from fear.
He is a refuge in time of doubt and trouble, he is light
and life. He rescues from the hand of enemies, lifts up
the downcast. He is a shelter, a rock, a fortress. He it is
who provides running waters for the thirsty, joy and
peace to the afflicted. He is merciful, he frees from sin
and confinement. In a vacillating world, he is a surety,
one who can be trusted in without fear of treachery or
disillusionment. To catalog all the reasons why Israel
longed to experience Yahweh and to see his face is virtually to rewrite the entire Old Testament.

One of the themes which underlies all of the ways in
which Yahweh is salvation, the end of man's desires, can
be found in the Hebrew word for salvation itself,
yeshu'ah (from which word *Jesus* is derived). The word
connotes freedom, the possession of open space, liberation from constraint and limitation. It is frequently
used in opposition to Hebrew words meaning narrow-
ness, being closed-in, cramped or impeded.

In these senses salvation is frequently identified with
life, and lack of salvation with death. Death itself is
described in terms of imprisonment: the bonds of death,
the pit from which there is no escape.

In the earlier Old Testament writings salvation and
life were conceived of in rather material terms: possession of the land, good health, an abundance of crops,
prosperity, freedom from enemies. Eventually, however, especially as depicted in some of the Psalms and in
the Book of Wisdom, life takes on a much broader,
richer meaning. One can be physically dead and yet
alive in this fuller sense: "To the foolish they seem
dead, but they are at peace . . . and their hope is full of

immortality." (Wis 3:2-4) Conversely, what more moving witness to the type of death experienced while physically alive than in the agonized cries of the psalmist, "I am lost among the dead, like the slain lying in their graves. Friend and lover you have taken from me, my only companion is the darkness." (Ps 88:6, 19)

It was this confinement, this death in life, that tormented Job. And it was in the hope of seeing God that Job foresaw his liberation: "I know that my Redeemer lives and that my Support shall stand upon the dust, and from my flesh I shall see God." (Job 19:25, 26b)

There is no man who does not in some way experience the confinement and limitation so vividly described in the Old Testament. Who of us does not cry out for freedom, to see our liberator standing upon the dust? Who, however he might imagine it, does not yearn to see the face of God?

One affliction, common to all man but especially acute in our stage of history, is the nagging doubt that our existence makes any difference. Billions of persons such as we are have come, gone, and are not remembered in the many millennia of man's presence on earth. Probably many billions more will anonymously come and go. And now in our brief moment we too seem faceless billions. Countless hundreds or thousands may be disposed of in a single war or natural disaster and are recalled only as a single headline or two the next day. Think of the tens of millions of Bengalis killed in 1970-1971 either in typhoons or in the civil war that followed. The country and the world go on, they are soon forgotten. Am I similarly to be understood as just one of millions who pass by?

The conspiracy of war and a general contempt for life forces an anonymity into our lives which gradually

eats away our sense of existence as individuals. I am
forced to mute the voice within that dares to say that I
am special, that with everything in and about me that
makes me to be what I am and what no one else is, I
have a wonderful and peculiar existence, that my life
means something, that it is going someplace—in short,
the voice that says that the fact that *I am* makes a difference to someone. We silence this voice, because in
the face of the facts it seems a cry of madness, an
unrealistic and unfulfillable illusion that only makes
life more difficult.

Vanity of vanities, and all is vanity.
What difference do a man's efforts
make under the sun?
One generation goes, another comes,
but the earth stays on forever.
Everything is full of weariness,
there is nothing man can say.
What has been, that is what will be.
What men have done, so will they do.
There is nothing new under the sun.
If someone says,
"Look! There is something new!"—
no, it has already been
in the ages that came before us.
There is no remembrance
of those who came before,
and for those yet to come,
there will be no remembrance
among their successors. (Eccl 1:3-11)

From this apparent entrapment in history we cry out
for release, but there are other confinements even more
personal to us from which we long for salvation, for
open space and freedom. We are in many ways prison-
ers of our own individual histories. Frequently we can-

not break out of the compulsive behavior patterns created by the fears and hurts of our past. As we perceive new and more significant goals, we find we have neither the psychic nor the physical energy to pursue them untrammeled by chains of the past. In new situations I am not totally free. Past doubts and fears creep out of the secret corners of my heart where they had lain hidden. I experience the terrible limitation of not being able to make my body and my spirit do exactly as I would bid them do. It is as St. Paul said, "I do not understand even my own actions. I do not do what I want to do, but rather the very thing I hate." (Rom 7:15)

All these things are the darkness which has become our companion in place of the friend and lover. But there is a sense in which even what is best and most beautiful within us leads to a cry: "When shall I be raised up from the dust to see the face of God?"

I recall a few years ago when one or another of our astronauts in orbit had broken free from the pull of the earth and soared out into the open toward the moon. As we watched the newscast, we felt an exhilaration, a sense of new freedom. The very thought of breaking out of our world into the beyond, of flying free into the infinite, awoke in us a deep-down longing for transcendence, a yearning to get beyond ourselves—now somehow spoken to symbolically in the astronaut's space feat.

The trouble is that man has built-in desires that leap beyond the possibilities of his now limited existence. More than anything else we want someone to say a total Yes to us. We want to be loved and accepted without reserve, not for what people think we are, but for what we really are. We want someone to reach into our hearts and see all the insecurities and darknesses, those little secrets we ourselves can never quite accept, and to say Yes, even in these hidden recesses you are wonderful as you are, I love you, I rejoice in everything I see.

Conversely we too wish totally to understand and love another. We cannot help it. No man is born to be alone, and the desire for union in unreserved acceptance and love operates throughout every major decision we make in our lives. When for some reason there is no hope for this fulfillment, when one feels definitively alone, there is no reason to live, and every day we read of those who on these grounds take the obvious step. Again it is the cry of the psalmist, "Friend and lover you have taken from me, my only companion is the darkness. I am shut up so that I cannot escape." (Ps 88:19, 9)

The more our love and understanding grow in this life and become a source of joy, the more they open to us a possibility and a desire that they themselves cannot satisfy. We are in many ways opaque and mysterious to ourselves. This opacity enters into every one of our relationships with another. I simply cannot take everything that I am and put it inside another, nor so take another into myself, since this giving and taking require total acceptance, which in turn means total understanding. If I cannot completely understand and accept myself, can I completely and unreservedly understand and accept another?

Yet as love grows, this total giving and taking becomes more and more the impossible imperative. In this way love can, ironically, make us lonely. We want too much. The union we desire now is so much deeper than that envisioned at the outset of the love relationship that the distance yet to go seems infinitely farther than the distance we foresaw in our less mature perspective.

It is often with this realization that we first reach out for God in a dark and undefined encounter. We begin to yearn for the complete correlative to our being, the one we *can* totally accept and love and who will totally accept and love us. We weary of seeing in a glass darkly, we wish to see face to face.

As we shall learn from St. John, this pursuit of God is not an escape from this world, from our human history, and least of all from our human love. On the contrary, it will be only in and through them that we will find our liberator standing upon the dust.

2. God Is Light

For St. John a man is in darkness if he is apart from God. If his longing for liberation and fulfillment remains active and makes him willing to risk, he will see over the horizon the true light coming into his world to dispel that lonely darkness, inviting him to a life and a love that go far beyond what he could have imagined or dared to hope for.

If he accepts that invitation he will find himself in a healing encounter with God. Like the woman at the well in John's narrative, he will begin to drink of living waters that will well up within him to everlasting life. If, however, like the Pharisees he has grown enured to his cramped world of fear, darkness and self-enclosure, the prospect of freedom poses for him only the unacceptable threat of the unknown, and he will reject the light, sensing that life and freedom mean love, and that love involves a self-emptying and a certain insecurity which he cannot face.

We shall see later that John implies that in a sense the man who accepts the light was already a son of the light, whereas the man who chooses to remain in the darkness makes himself even in his past history a son of darkness. This, on examination, is not some sort of determinism, but a profound insight into the fact that our personal histories are *continua:* what we affirm of our future we make our past also to be.

What we wish to pursue at this point is John's picture of a man without God, man tied down to his own limitations. John's vocabulary tends to be the same, whether he is describing a man before he sees the light or a man who has been presented with the light and rejects it. Both, although for different reasons, are in the darkness.

John uses the image of darkness over a dozen times. The metaphorical use of darkness in the Old Testament is rather common. The psalmist we cited in the previous chapter used the expression to articulate the overwhelming alienation and isolation he experienced in his confinement: "Friend and lover you have taken from me, my only companion is the darkness." (Ps 88:19) So also, Job cries out in his misery, "I had hoped for light, but the darkness came." (Job 30:26)

In the figurative language of the Genesis creation accounts, which language John very consciously echoes in the prologue to his Gospel, the negative forces in and about man are alternately depicted as chaos or darkness. It is noteworthy that in the Priestly account of creation God symbolically creates light *within* the darkness in such a way that the darkness remains, but it is circumscribed and manageable; man has darkness in his life from the beginning, but he finds control over it and liberation from it in the light of God's creative activity.

When in the Yahwist narration of the fall man has set himself apart from God, the dark forces that had been held in check now well up against him unto death, vitiating all that had seemed most precious to him. Although the greatest joy for man is in love and human union, even this now must be tinged with pain. There is the suggestion to Eve that not only will childbirth, the fulfillment of her love, be mingled with tears, but even the love relationship with her husband itself will be radically ambiguous. Sexuality will be as much a source of confusion as it will be of ecstasy. And instead of being in joyful harmony with the universe about him, man now experiences a brooding alienation from it. Man was created in life, and now he is dust. Unto dust he shall return.

John delineates more carefully this image of man apart from God, isolated within his narrowed possibilities. Because he stumbles in the darkness, he can see and understand neither himself nor his brother. The experience of real love and communication, toward which he tends by nature, is precluded from his life. His incarnation becomes the obfuscation of his spirit rather than the lucid expression of it. Everything within him calls out for transcendence, yet he clings to fleeting chimeras. Because he has not been liberated in the love that casts out fear, his life is shadowed by doubt and insecurity, especially as to the ultimate worth of his own existence. In a word, his is a living death.

It could not be otherwise. God himself *is* life and love. Without God there can be an experience of neither life nor love, and vice versa.

(We should note here that when John speaks of *God,* he means the Father. Although some of what we shall shortly speak of as coming from God John more specifically attributes to the Son, everything that comes through the Son is ultimately from the Father, and, in fact, the distinctions which John makes in the Gospel concerning the operations of the Father and the Son are not so clear in the First Letter.)

If man left on his own is in darkness, God is the light that shines through that darkness. In this light man discovers a new and transcendent principle of activity. God cuts through the opacity of our earthliness and takes away our blindness, enabling us not only to know, understand and accept ourselves, but to see into and love our brothers and to allow them to see into and love us, since the light drives out fears and phantoms.

This light is life, not just an upward extension of the rather two-dimensional life of man on his own resources, but the transcendent inner life of God himself reaching down into our death-riddled life and raising us beyond our intrinsic capacities, pulling us toward an ever deeper union with him, and through him with all men. From the dust of unfulfilled anonymity we are led to such a freedom that at the comsummation of our history "we shall see him as he is, and we shall be like him." (1 Jn 3:2) Not only will our longing to see the face of God be realized, but the encounter will totally transform us.

John describes this historical fulfillment not as a sudden intervention, as if this present life were a sullen period of waiting for release from the miseries of this world. Rather it is the fruition of a process that begins the moment one enters into the light that comes to every man if he will receive it. There is a rebirth *now,* not in the flesh, but in the fire of the Spirit. There is a force which works not to destruction, but to eternal life. A man will drink this water and never thirst again, eat this food and never hunger again.

Breaking through metaphors John consistently labels this process as a love affair with God. As we grow in love, the veil is gradually removed from his face, and we become like him. God is love.

Having said all this, are we not still left with the problem we began with? We knew in the beginning, really, that in some way God was our fulfillment. But do we not still reach out desperately like Job, not knowing where to find him? Where is this God? How do we have access to him?

3. The Word Was with God

Almost everything we will reflect on in this chapter can be found in germ in the remarkable greeting of John's First Letter:

What was from the beginning,
what we have heard,
what we have seen with our eyes,
what we have looked on
and touched with our hands—
it is the Word of Life.

This Life became manifest.
We have seen it and bear witness to it,
and we proclaim to you the eternal Life
which was present to the Father
and was made manifest to us.

What we have seen and heard
we proclaim also to you,
so that you may have fellowship with us.
Our fellowship is with the Father
and with his Son, Jesus Christ. (1 Jn 1:1-3)

What John is saying is this: all that the Father is, here summed up as *Life,* is in Jesus Christ made touchable, hearable, seeable. The reality of the Father is expressed and made manifest in Jesus.

The use of *Word* in this context is not so determinate as it is in the prologue to the Gospel. Here it seems to mean the outward manifestation of Life which is experienced in Jesus. In the Gospel prologue it is explicitly identified with Jesus himself: he *is* the incarnate manifestation of all that the Father is:

In the beginning was the Word,
and the Word was in God's presence,
and the Word was God.
He was present to God in the beginning.
All things came to be through him,
and apart from him nothing came to be.
In him was Life,
and the Life was the light of men. . . .

And the Word became flesh and dwelled among us,
and we have seen his glory,
glory as of the only Son of the Father,
full of grace and truth. (Jn 1:1-4, 14)

The two ideas come to pretty much the same thing, and in subsequent passages in the Gospel John alternates the emphasis, sometimes using language which suggests that what the Father is can be experienced through Jesus, sometimes language that says more concretely that Jesus is himself that reality now made accessible through the incarnation.

Let us examine some expressions in the prologue more closely. Some have sought to explain John's use of *Word* (*logos* in Greek) by reference to the philosophical literature of the contemporary Hellenistic world. There *logos* is frequently a principle of order or intelligibility, reason, and the like. John may not reject these connotations, since they would evoke certain passages in Old Testament wisdom literature with which he was clearly familiar. In general, however, one must turn to a more specifically Hebraic thought-world to understand *Word* in John, especially since he rather obviously intends to echo many key Old Testament themes and passages in the prologue—as he does, indeed, throughout the Gospel.

Logos translates the Hebrew *davar*. (*Davar* in its various verbal and nominal forms is used more than 2,500 times in the Old Testament.) *Davar* in Hebrew is not exactly *word* in our sense, although *word* is the most common translation used in Old Testament versions. More exactly, a *davar* is an external manifestation or expression of a personality, whether in word, act, or even in appearance. If you wish to know what sort of person a man is, look at him, observe what he does, listen to what he says. These things are all Hebrew *words*.

In this sense the Law is a word of Yahweh, since it reveals his holiness and how he may be encountered in man's activity. Creation, all of nature, and the process of history are words of Yahweh, since in them he makes himself known. The Priestly account of creation, for example, sees God as embodying his glory in the work of his hands. The Yahwist account sees man and his universe as manifesting God's creative love.

We read in the Book of Wisdom:

If men were amazed at the power and energy [within the wonders of creation], let them learn from them how much more powerful is he who made them. For from the greatness and beauty of created things comes an analogous perception of their creator. (Wis 13:4-5)

Creation reveals God because he has sent out his creative word and it continues to speak on in its handiwork:

The heavens declare the glory of God,
and the firmament proclaims his handiwork.

Day pours forth speech to day,
and night to night declares knowledge.
There is no speech, there are no words
whose voice is not heard.
Through all the earth their voice goes out,
and to the ends of the world their message. (Ps 19:2-5)

In Hebrew thought the word, once it proceeds from
the person, takes on a quasi-independent reality of its
own. The word not only has meaning in that it reveals
the person who utters it, but has its own interior dynamism which brings about the reality it signifies. It
somehow expands and concretizes exteriorly the being
of the person who spoke it.

Hence we read of curses and blessings in the Old Testament which once spoken are irrevocable, since a new
reality has come into being, a release and extension of
interior power, which cannot be withdrawn. Thus it was
with Isaac's blessing of Jacob, originally intended for
his brother Esau. (Gen 27:1-40)

Similarly with the prophetic word: the prophet receives the word from Yahweh not just as a message to
be conveyed to the people, but as a burning reality
which embodies the compelling personality of Yahweh.
In the word the prophet encounters the holiness and
power of Yahweh himself. It was for this reason that
Jeremiah could not run away from his prophetic mandate:

You have seduced me, Yahweh,
and I have let myself be seduced.
You were too strong for me,
and you have prevailed.
All day I am a laughingstock,
everyone is mocking me.
For every time I utter the word, I cry out;

I proclaim violence and destruction.
For the word of Yahweh has meant nothing to me
but daily insult and derision.
If I say "I won't think about him,
I won't speak any more in his name,"
then there is something in my heart
like a burning fire,
imprisoned in my bones.
I am too weary to hold it in,
I cannot restrain it. (Jer 20:7-9)

The theme of the inexorability of God's word and the tendency to view the word as a reality on its own are brought together in Deutero-Isaiah:

Just as the rain and snow
come down from heaven
and do not return there,
but water the earth,
making it to bear and to be fruitful,
giving seed to the sower,
bread to the eater,
so it is with the word
that goes forth from my mouth.
It shall not return to me empty,
but shall accomplish my will,
achieving the purpose
for which I sent it. (Is 55:10-11)

Finally, the word is the instrument of creation: "By the word of Yahweh the heavens were made, by the breath of his mouth all their hosts." (Ps 33:6) Yahweh utters his creative word which accomplishes his handi-work, embodying itself in the created things as the living manifestation of their maker. The creative word does not cease to be, but speaks on in the universe.

Let us return now to the prologue of John's Gospel in a sort of paraphrase. The Father eternally speaks his

Word, the Son. He is the perfect manifestation of the Father. As the Father is Life, so the Son is Life. The Father created all things through his Word, the Son. As in the Genesis account God's creative word does not cease to be with creation, but enters into it as a manifestation of God's glory, so the Son, at a point in man's history, enters into creation, taking on the flesh of man, thereby giving man access to the reality of the Father from within. In Jesus, the God-man, we experience the glory of the Father. It cannot be overstressed that creation and the incarnation constitute one linear unfolding of the Word of God.

It is not impossible that when John says, "[The Word] came to his own, but his people did not receive him" (Jn 1:11), he is referring not only to Jesus' ministry, but to the role of Word in Old Testament prophecy before the incarnation. This thought is explicit in 1 Peter: "The prophets prophesied . . . by the Spirit of Christ within them when predicting the sufferings of Christ and the subsequent glory." (1 Pet 1:10-11) There is thus a progressive realization of the Word uttered by the Father: the eternal Word with the Father, the creative Word, the prophetic Word, the incarnate Word.

Although this "Word-theology" is characteristically Johannine, there is a close parallel to it in Paul's Letter to the Colossians:

Christ is the image of the invisible God, the firstborn of all creation, because in him all things were created, in heaven and on earth. . . . All things were created through him and for him. . . . In him all the fullness of God was pleased to dwell. . . . He is the mystery hidden from ages and generations but now made manifest. . . . In him the fullness of deity dwells bodily. (Col 1:15-16a, 19, 26; 2:9)

John underscores the theme that we have access to the Father in Jesus, the incarnate Word, by saying, "We have seen his glory, glory as of the only son of the Father." (Jn 1:14) In the Old Testament *glory* (Hebrew *kavod,* Greek *doxa*) was the visible manifestation of Yahweh's presence when he acted in power among his people. This glory is sometimes described as smoke and fire, sometimes as a cloud filling the tabernacle, most characteristically, however, as a brilliant light, often shining through a cloud.

The dynamic presence of Yahweh which gives rise to this externalization of his glory is called his *shekinah,* "indwelling," in early rabbinic literature. John apparently intends a pun on this word in his choice of words for *dwelled* in "He [i.e., the Word] dwelled among us." He chooses a form of the unexpected Greek verb *skenoun* which means literally "to tent." The *s-k-n* pun between *shekinah* and the Greek verb may seem far-fetched to the modern reader, but such word-plays abound in the Scriptures.

Jesus, then, as the incarnate Word of God, is God's presence in power among his people, and the glory of the invisible God is made visible in Jesus. "No one has ever seen God. It is God the only Son, who is in the bosom of the Father, who has revealed him." (Jn 1:18)

A similar thought is found in Paul: "All men have sinned and are deprived of the glory of God . . . but God made Christ Jesus the propitiatory." (Rom 3:23, 25a) The propitiatory was the gold lid which covered the ark of the covenant in the Old Testament. It symbolized Yahweh's throne when he was present with the people. What Paul is saying is that man on his own is deprived of the liberating presence of God, but through God's sending of his Son, God is present to man in power.

The Letter to the Hebrews puts it this way:

In times past God spoke to our fathers through the prophets in many and different ways. But now, in these last days, he has spoken to us through his Son, whom he has made the heir of all things, and through whom he also created the universe. The Son is the reflection of God's glory, the exact representation of what God is, sustaining all things with his word of power. (Heb 1:1-3a)

In summary, the God whom man longs to see and to experience for his liberation from darkness may be encountered in Jesus, God's Word, who is God made manifest and accessible in the flesh—seeable, touchable, hearable.

Let us now pursue the implications of this theme, seeking to discover more precisely the nature and mode of this possible encounter with God in Jesus.

4. You Shall Know the Truth

Jesus the incarnate Word is everything the Father is but made manifest and accessible to man. When an individual encounters this reality of the Father in Jesus, John speaks of *truth*. Truth refers either to this reality of the Father as it can be experienced, to the experience itself, or to the effects of the experience. Let me explain.

Truth is not the opposite of falsehood in St. John's writings. Rather it is opposed to sin and darkness. John does use the truth-lie opposition on occasion, especially in the First Letter, but even here *lie,* a natural verbal correlative to *truth,* means more broadly that which is without God or which acts in opposition to him.

Underlying the use of much of the biblical vocabulary that deals with knowing or perceiving (*truth, see, know, knowledge, notice, realize,* even *believe* and *belief*) is the idea of an encounter with a reality, usually an interpersonal encounter. In a passage of the Book of Wisdom we cited previously, pagans are chided because, while deriving useful knowledge from observing the wonders of the universe, they were blind to the fact that they were thereby involved in an interpersonal encounter with God:

All men were foolish by nature who were ignorant of God, and who from the good things that are seen did not succeed in knowing him who is, and did not recognize the craftsman while studying his works. (Wis 13:1)

24

Knowing for the Hebrew was not so much an intellectual grasp of something as it was a total personal experience of it—whence the "heart" was said to be the seat of knowing—such as in the English usage "to know pain" or "I have known hard times." The experience described as *knowing* may assume a variety of refinements having to do with the relationship between the person encountering and the object or other person encountered. Thus "to know nothing about something" means not to be concerned with or to take care of it. In Psalm 50:11 Yahweh says: "I know all the birds of the air, and all that stirs in the fields is mine," where *knowing* involves possessing and having control over. To "know a woman" is to have sexual intercourse with her. To "know sin" is not to have an intellectual appreciation of what evil is, but to live in a world of darkness where evil is an operative force in man's life. Not to know God is not so much an error of judgment as it is a rejection of him.

Finally, to "know God" is to accept him into one's life, to believe in him, to have a mutual relationship with him. In speaking of the conversion from idolatry to Yahweh, Deuteronomy speaks of a total, personally involved relationship with Yahweh and then labels this relationship "knowing": "You will seek Yahweh and you will find him, if you search after him with your whole heart and your whole soul. . . . Know then and put it in your heart, that Yahweh is God in heaven above and on the earth below; there is no other." (Deut 4:29, 39)

John also uses *know* in this way. "This is eternal life, that they know you, [Father], and Jesus Christ whom you have sent." (Jn 17:3) "I am the good shepherd. I know my own and mine know me." (Jn 9:14) Sometimes, as in Deuteronomy, *to know* and *to love* seem almost to merge in concept, especially when Jesus describes his relationship with the Father.

Truth, to know the truth and similar expressions, however, are more typically Johannine ways of designating the transforming relationship with the Father, especially as made possible in and experienced through Jesus. The interplay between knowledge, truth and love is richly expressed in a passage from the First Letter:

By this may we be sure that we have come to know him, if we keep his commandments. If anyone says "I have come to know him," but does not keep his commandments, he is a liar and the truth is not in him. But whoever keeps his word, truly the love of God has been made perfect in him. By this we may be sure that we are in him: he who says he abides in him ought to walk in the same way he walked. (1 Jn 2:3-5)

Clearly we are dealing here not with keeping score on intellectually accumulated facts, but with a whole way of life, a being caught up into a personal and liberating relationship with God in Jesus, and acting accordingly.

When Jesus says "I am the Way, the Truth and the Life" (Jn 14:6a), he is saying: if you seek the Father, I am your access to him (Way). In fact I am the experience of the Father (Truth), because I am myself the very reality (Life) you are seeking in the Father. Jesus himself gives this explanation of the statement: "No one comes to the Father except through me. If you really knew me, you would know my Father also. From this point on you do know him—you have seen him!" (Jn 14:6b-7)

Philip, to whom Jesus is addressing this declaration, still does not grasp the force of Jesus' words. Like the psalmist he is stirred with the thought of seeing the

Father—"I thirst for God, for the living God. When shall I go and behold the face of God?" (Ps 42:2) But he seems now to expect that Jesus might be on the brink of staging some dramatic Sinai-like theophany, not quite believing that the Father can really be encountered in Jesus. "Lord, show us the Father and we shall be satisfied." (Jn 14:8) Jesus answers him:

Have I been with you so long and you have not come to know me? Whoever has seen me has seen the Father! How can you then say "Show us the Father"? Do you not believe that I am in the Father and the Father is in me? What I say to you I do not say of myself. The Father who dwells in me is doing his own works. Believe me that I am in the Father and the Father is in me, or else believe because of the works themselves. (Jn 14:9-11)

If one experiences the Father in Jesus, and assents to this experience in faith (we have not yet discussed the dynamics of faith), he is said to "be of the truth" or to "walk in the light." Darkness and death are dispelled from his life: "I am the light of the world. Whoever follows me will never walk in the darkness, but will have the light of life." (Jn 8:12)

In a word, Jesus is liberation. In him the believer is no longer a slave of his past nor doomed to an unfulfilled future. Man's desire to leap beyond the bonds of his limitations, to be freed from faceless anonymity, to know that his life has a meaning and a future, his desire to love and to be loved without fear and misunderstand—God takes these longings in the encounter with him in Jesus with the promise of fulfillment, not some hidden distant fulfillment, but one that begins in the encounter itself, soaring to its consummation when finally "we shall be like him, for we shall see him as he is." (1

Jn 3:2) "If you remain in my word," Jesus tells those
who had come to believe in him, "you are truly my fol-
lowers. And you shall know the truth, and the truth will
set you free!" (Jn 8:31-32)

Philip's problem was that his vision was not able to
penetrate beyond the limited dimensions of his past experience. Like the pseudo-scientists of Wisdom 13, he
could not grasp the transcendent reality that was at
work in what he saw and heard. "Have you been with
me so long and you have not come to know me? Whoever has seen me has seen the Father!" (Jn 14:9)

Throughout John's Gospel narrative Jesus is at pains
patiently to lead those who encounter him into this
higher vision, that is, to know the truth, to have a liberating experience of the Father in himself. This transforming leap of insight is, as we shall see in some detail
later, the work of the Spirit, and is equivalently a new
birth since it involves entrance into life of a new order.
The leap is not so much a sudden growth in intellectual
apprehension as it is a falling in love.

Take the example of a young man who has dated a
girl for several months. He knows virtually all the
"facts" about her life—her background, the number
and names of the members of her family, her likes and
dislikes, etc. After a time, all the details are filled in—
what she has read, her political views, and so on. Then
one day it happens—he falls in love with her. Suddenly
half of the "facts" he knew about her become virtually
irrelevant. Through being in love, he now knows her in
a way that goes far beyond the way he knew her before.
Love caused a jump from a catalog of loosely connect-
ed data to a unified insight into a person.

As I am writing this, I am thinking about a friend of
mine I love very much. There are an enormous number

of "facts" others know about him which I do not, but because I love him, I am convinced that I know him better than almost anyone else. For one thing, I recognize something in him that is intrinsically very exciting and beautiful. I suppose this would be true in anyone, since people are by nature exciting and beautiful, but love gives us that peculiar type of affective insight that enables us to see this wonderful thing in someone and to rejoice in it.

When Nicodemus tells Jesus, "We know you are a teacher who has come from God, since no one can perform the signs you do unless God is with him," Jesus tells him that that is not enough. Nicodemus has not yet adequately burst free from the confines of his earthly vision (Nicodemus "came to him *at night*") truly to grasp in love the magnitude of the reality he is encountering in Jesus. "I tell you, [Nicodemus], unless a man is born from above, he cannot *see* the kingdom of God." (Jn 3:3)

John makes frequent use of irony to bring out the contrast between the limited reality man has come to accept as normative and the limitless reality of God which is offered to him in Jesus. Thus in the phrase "unless a man is born from above," the word for "from above" (Greek *anothen*) can also mean "again," and this is the way Nicodemus understands it. He asks Jesus, "How can a man be born when he is old? Can he enter his mother's womb and be born a second time?" Jesus then makes the contrast involved in his original statement more explicit: "What is born of the flesh is flesh, what is born of the Spirit is spirit." (Jn 3:4, 6)

So with the woman at the well. Jesus promises her "living water." "If only you had recognized God's gift and who it is who is speaking with you, you would have

asked him and he would have given you living water."
She takes "living water" to mean simply "flowing
water" as opposed to the stale water of cisterns: "Sir,
you have nothing to draw with, and the well is deep.
Where do you get living (= flowing) water?" But what
Jesus intended by "living water" was "water of Life":
"Everyone who drinks the water [of this well] will be
thirsty again, but whoever drinks the water I give him
will never thirst again. No, the water I shall give him
will become a fountain within him, welling up to eternal
life." (Jn 4:10-11, 13-14)

It is also the major function of the *signs* in John's
Gospel to reveal through Jesus' symbolic actions the
person he is and the nature of the salvation offered to
men by the Father in Jesus. Jesus, for example, grants
life to the official's dying son but later indicates the revelation that actually lay behind such a cure:

Just as the Father raises the dead and gives them life,
so the Son gives life to whom he wishes. He who hears
my word and has faith in him who sent me, possesses
eternal life. He does not come under condemnation, but
has passed from death to life." (Jn 5:21, 24)

Jesus cures the man born blind, and this is the ex-
change that follows between Jesus and the Pharisees,
who reviled the youth for believing in Jesus:

Jesus said, "I came into this world for judgment, so
that those who are blind may see and those who see
may become blind." Some of the Pharisees near him
heard this and said, "Are you saying that we are
blind?" Jesus answered them, "If you were really blind,
you would have no sin. But since you say 'We see,' your
sin remains." (Jn 9:39-41)

Curing physical blindness was a sign of giving a new

spiritual vision. The Pharisees claim to have adequate spiritual vision, but since they are hypocritical in their assertion, Jesus says that they are in fact voluntarily blind. This is none other than the earlier theme of darkness and light.

Similarly, when Jesus, in answer to the pleas of Martha and Mary, was about to raise their brother Lazarus from the dead, he gradually elicited from Martha a confession that she saw beyond the event to the reality it was revealing.

Martha said to Jesus, "Lord, if you had been here, my brother would not have died. But I know that whatever you ask of God, God will give to you." Jesus said to her, "Your brother will rise again." "I know he will rise again in the resurrection on the last day," Martha replied. Jesus said to her, "*I am* the Resurrection and the Life. Whoever believes in me, even if he die, shall live. Whoever is alive and believes in me shall never die. Do you believe this?" She answered him, "Yes, Lord. I have come to believe that you are the Messiah, the Son of God, he who is coming into the world." (Jn 11:21-27)

John's message in summary is this: Man longs to reach out of his darkness into the light, to rise above death to life. He wishes to experience God who is Light and Life himself. He knows that in God he will be liberated from the weight of his unfulfilled hopes and terrible limitations. If one is willing to take the risk of love, to step out of his secure but overshadowed world, he may experience God in the God-man Jesus, incarnate Word of the Father. Little by little in this encounter he will be delivered from his bonds, set soaringly free in a way that goes beyond his most daring hope. This deliverance is not simply a promise held out for some distant future, but a process that takes hold the moment of the encounter with Jesus. "You shall know the truth and the truth will set you free!"

Whoever believes in me believes not so much in me as in him who sent me. And whoever looks on me is really seeing him who sent me. I have come Light into the world, that whoever believes in me may not remain in the darkness. (Jn 12:44-46)

5. The Word Became Flesh

At this point I can see you raising at least two very legitimate questions. First, we have elaborated the theme that the Word became flesh, that the Son of God became man as we are men. But really, in stressing that in Jesus there is the transcendental reality of the Father present, Jesus being the Truth and the Life, haven't we done away with the humanity of Jesus? It might seem that Jesus were some mysterious force hovering untouchable among men, but not really man at all in any sense of that word that means anything to us. One could picture him as unperturbable and detached, moving slowly and deliberately, always in command of every situation, and speaking to those who followed him with an expressionless face, often closed eyes, and with terribly lofty, awesome words. It would appear that God became man in name only, that he was never really "one of us."

Secondly, it is all well and good to talk about having access to God in Jesus, to speak of "encounters" with him. But let's be honest, Jesus isn't around. He's been gone for almost two thousand years, hasn't he? For the man born blind and the woman at the well Jesus was there to encounter, but—face it—he isn't here anymore. Are we supposed to put ourselves piously in the past and play a prayer game of let's-pretend? Are we, as some old meditation books suggested, to "place yourself in Galilee and imagine Jesus standing before you;

what do you say to him, etc.?"

Actually these two questions, we shall see, reduce to one, and both have to do with the nature of the incarnation as part of the process of the unfolding of God's word. There may also be a bit of a hidden agenda lurking behind both questions, especially the first, in the form of the unspoken suspicion: maybe God doesn't really love us.

Knowing how many persons, things and situations we ourselves regard with less than enthusiasm in our day-to-day lives, and how difficult we find it to be unreservedly committed even to those we love, we tend to doubt that God really cares all that much and all that intimately about us and our world. Although we may be told repeatedly otherwise, it's hard to escape the feeling sometimes that God is sufficiently detached so that he really doesn't want to get inextricably involved in our affairs. If we're good, he'll reward us; if not, well. . . .

Since this uneasy thought is with all of us at some time or other, and since dispelling it is so very necessary in order to put the incarnation (and the answer to our two questions) into the right perspective, it will not be amiss to devote a bit of time to this matter. Unless we are convinced that God takes human history very seriously indeed, it will be very difficult for us to take it seriously ourselves.

The two Genesis accounts of creation employ imagery which shows a profound insight into God's attitude toward the world he creates, especially toward man. In both versions God seems almost to be bursting with enthusiasm. It reminds me of a common experience many of us have had. Picture yourself sitting alone in your room reading when suddenly you come to a beautiful, stirring passage. It says something just right. You can't wait to read it to someone. You may even run out into the hallway to see if there is someone there to share it with.

Better yet, remember that wonderful thing that happens to you when you fall in love—you want to shout it from the rooftops for all to hear.

This is the atmosphere that surrounds the poetical creation stories of Genesis. God freely wishes to share his beauty and goodness with someone who can appreciate it and rejoice in it. We have mentioned before that in the first account there is an emphasis on God's pouring out his glory and dominion to be shared, in the second, his love. God is lavish with his gifts to man, and after each step of creation God sees the work of his hands and says "It is good!" Man, intended to rejoice with God in his goodness, "God created in his own image, in the divine image he created him."

God's intimate relationship with man and his loving concern for him are expressed in bold anthropomorphisms: he makes man to live by breathing in his nostrils his own breath, he presents woman to man as a gift, he walks in their garden in the cool of the evening.

It must be stressed over and over that God's creative stance of love for and intimacy with man never changes on his part, since God is love itself:

Beloved, let us love one another,
because love is of God.
Everyone who loves
is born of God and knows God.
The man without love does not know God,
because God is love.

This is how God's love was revealed in us:
he sent his only Son into the world

that we might have life through him.

This is love, then,
not that we have loved God,
but that God has loved us,
and has sent his Son
as the expiation for our sins. (1 Jn 4:7-10)

    Even when man sins, God continues to love. Sin is by definition a refusal to accept a gift from God, and even if man turns away and will not receive that gift, God's hand is still extended in love. Rather, by sin a man alienates himself from the world about him, and even from his own deepest desires. This alienation is frequently expressed anthropomorphically in the Old Testament as "God's wrath," but in reality it is our own wrath against ourselves. God remains ever in love with us. " 'Do I take pleasure in the death of the wicked?' says the Lord. 'Do I not rather rejoice when he turns from his evil way that he might live?' " (Ez 18:23)

You are merciful to all men
because you can do all things.
You overlook men's sins,
that they may know conversion.

For you love everything that is
and loathe nothing you have made.
If you had hated anything,
you would not have created it.

How could anything have endured
if you had not willed it so?
Or how have been preserved
if not called forth by you?

Yes, you forbear all things
because they all are yours,
O Lord who loves the living. (Wis 11:23-26)

When we turn from our blindness, we see God still offering us the gift of his love. We speak of this as forgiveness or pardon, but this does not mean that God was angry and then relented, although Scripture poetically attributes these ways to God, by analogy to the human situation of a father being "angry" with his child precisely because he loves him.

It has not generally been noticed that in the Genesis story of the sin of Adam and Eve, if one considers honestly the anthropomorphic style, God does not really punish them, but rather pronounces what is simply a *fait accompli:* because man has rejected in some way God's gift of creation (it is not clear what sin is symbolized in the apple and serpent motif), man is now in jarring disharmony with creation and within himself. God acknowledges this and, if anything, tries to help Adam and Eve in their confused state. Because sex is now partially an embarrassment to them, God fashions clothes for them. When God drives them from the tree of life in paradise, his motive seems primarily to protect them from doing even greater harm to themselves.

Because we ourselves turn negatively against those who do not accept us or our gifts, because we hold grudges, and above all because we cannot really accept ourselves as lovable, we find it terribly difficult to believe that God, who is love, has an unqualified love for us. We seem almost morbidly to feel better if we can imagine God as being angry with us. It is very humbling to be loved when we feel we are not lovable. That means that we are put squarely on the receiving end, and therefore lose manipulative control of the situation. It is far more difficult to receive than to give.

But as Saints John and Paul insist, it is precisely in giving us gifts while we are self-alienated from him as sinners—even if we should continue to refuse those gifts —that he demonstrates the unqualified nature of his love for us.

God is, then, unremittingly enamored with us, our history and the world. If we freely choose to reject the gift he offers us, which is primarily the gift to be caught up in his love, he does not condemn us to darkness, we condemn ourselves. He continues being what he is, love, willing to befriend us intimately in a way we never seem willing to receive.

God so loved the world that he gave his only Son, that whoever believes in him should not perish, but have everlasting life. For God did not send the Son into the world to condemn the world, but that the world might be saved through him. Whoever believes in him is not condemned, but whoever does not believe is already condemned for not believing in the name of God's only Son. (Jn 3:16-18)

Man is not an embarrassment to God. You are not embarrassed by people you love. In fact, the more things seem to go wrong for them, the more you try to enter into their lives to bring healing: "The more sin increased, so much more did grace surpass it." (Rom 5:20)

If God has such a love affair with us, it should not be surprising then that he sent his Son to become truly man, to enter into our history as one of us, "like his brethren in every respect, tempted as we are, but without sin." (Heb 2:17; 4:15) Nor when incarnate did the

Word keep aloof from the condition of the human race he entered. "Though his state was divine, he did not regard equality with God as something to cling to, but emptied himself to assume the condition of a slave, being born as men are." (Phil 2:6-7)

Now it is true that whereas the Synoptic Gospels and the Letter to the Hebrews perhaps delineate in more detail the humanity which the Word assumed, John lays more stress on the nature of the Word who assumed it. Yet it is John who says, "Many deceitful ones have gone out into the world, men who will not acknowledge Jesus Christ as coming in the flesh. Such a one is a deceiver, an antichrist!" (2 Jn 7) John describes in moving terms the deep personal friendships of Jesus: with John himself, "the disciple whom Jesus loves" (Jn 13:23), with Martha, Mary and their brother Lazarus. When Lazarus died Jesus was "deeply troubled" and wept openly, leading those who stood about to whisper, "See how much he loved him!" (Jn 11:33-36) In John's Gospel Jesus is not just man in appearance, he is real flesh and blood. He could become righteously angry, he grew weary from his labors. What is more, Jesus had to face not only the death that comes to every man, but a most ignominious death. As the forces leading to this crisis became apparent to him, Jesus knew the profound agony of free decision.

In short, there is no doubt from John's Gospel that the incarnation was real. God actually did so love the world that he sent his Son to be one of us, God's word becoming ever more explicit to us and within our race in one continuous process of God's love unfolding: uttered by the Father in eternity, spoken in and through creation, working in the heart and on the lips of the prophets, finally become truly man, sharing in all things human but sin.

We must now pursue the second question we posed at the beginning of this chapter. The point we will wish to make is that the unfolding of the word did not stop with the incarnation, but reaches out into our history through every man who walks in his light—the extension of the incarnation in space and time.

6. My Father Glorifies Me

Through the incarnation God did not just come *to* the world, he came *into* the world. When God spoke his creative word in the beginning, that word did not "return to him empty," but in a sense entered into creation and continued to speak, revealing the glory and love of God. Creation is an ongoing process, a continual speaking of the word.

So also when the Word became flesh and dwelled among us. The Word did not come tangentially to the world, touching it on the surface at a moment in our history, then returning whence he came. No, through the flesh the Word irrupted into our history, penetrating the fiber of our human existence, irrevocably transforming it from within.

That is why we must carefully set aside the view of history which would say that Jesus came to us in the incarnation, left us a blueprint for achieving our reward, and died to make the reward possible, then left us at the ascension—to be met again only at the last judgment to requite us according to our deeds. If this were the case, it would mean that nothing has really happened to us, save that when we are finished with this life we will have the possibility for a fitting recompense since Jesus promised it to us. It would mean that we suffer patiently in this life, not because suffering and being human have some new internal dynamism and meaning, but because at the end, if we have remained virtuous in spite of it all, God will make it up to us in heaven.

In order to understand John's perspective of the internal change that takes place in mankind because of the incarnation, we must return to the idea of glory which we touched on briefly in Chapter Three.

Glory is the outward and discernible manifestation of the majestic presence of God in power. The Word uttered by God, whether eternal, creative, prophetic or incarnate, embodies the glory of God. John, you will recall, stressed that the reality of the Father was accessible and visible in his incarnate Word, Jesus, by saying, "We have seen his glory, glory as of the only Son of the Father." (Jn 1:14)

There is a parallel between the embodiment and manifestation of God's powerful presence, that is, his glory, in creation and in the incarnation. As we have said, when God creates through his Word, the Word enters into creation and continues to speak to the beholder, whence creation is full of the glory of God:

The heavens declare the glory of God,
and the firmament proclaims his handiwork.
Day pours forth speech to day,
and night to night
declares knowledge. (Ps 19:2-3)

In the incarnation the Word enters the weak flesh of man and takes it to himself, becoming like us in all things but sin. But because of the dynamic operation of the Word working within the humanity of Jesus by virtue of the incarnation, the glory of God is poured out into Jesus' humanity itself, and it becomes more and more a transformed reality, ever more capable of manifesting the presence of God. Since Jesus has a body like the rest of us, that body was doomed to death. But because of the power of the Word—"In the Word was Life" (1 Jn 1:4)—the death of Jesus' body is turned into the victory of the resurrection. As glory becomes decisively manifest in the humanity of Jesus, it flows from his humanity to all humanity, since we are, by the Spirit, in solidarity with Jesus, the God-man. (We shall speak of the Spirit later.) His victory is our victory.

The reality of the Father was manifest in Jesus' humanity from the beginning, and one could encounter it there. (Recall our earlier remarks on *truth*.) Jesus was constantly leading those who met him to this vision: Nicodemus, the woman at the well, Philip, Martha. From the moment of the incarnation Jesus had glory.

This glory, the sign of the Father's presence in the incarnate Word, was not *fully* present at the beginning however. It was only in the living out of his humanity unto death that the glory was fully revealed and humanity as such caught up in its transcendence. The glory of Jesus shone out in a progressively more heightened fashion in his works and "signs" as Jesus pursued his earthly ministry of revealing the Father. Jesus very frequently specifies that it is his Father working through him in these instances, and the glory of the Father that is being revealed in his acts.

"The Father who sent me bears witness to me." [The Pharisees] said to him, "Where is this Father of yours?" Jesus answered, "You know neither me nor my Father. If you knew me you would know my Father also. . . . If I am not doing the works of my Father, don't believe me. But if I am doing them, even if you don't believe me, believe the works themselves, so that you may realize that the Father is in me and I am in the Father." (Jn 8:18b-19; 10:37-38)

Jesus is even more explicit in his dialogue with Philip:

What I say to you I do not say of myself. The Father who dwells in me is doing his own works. Believe me that I am in the Father and the Father is in me, or else believe because of the works themselves. (Jn 14:10b-11)

Jesus ties together the works of the Father done through him with the revelation of glory: "If I glorify myself, my glory is nothing. It is my Father who glorifies me." (Jn 8:54) Glory comes "from the only God," (Jn 5:44) and in doing the Father's works, Jesus spreads his glory on earth.

When Jesus performs the sign at Cana, John reflects: "This was the first sign Jesus worked, and it revealed his glory, and his disciples believed in him." (Jn 2:11) Jesus, about to raise Lazarus from the dead, says, "His sickness is not to end in death, but it is for the glory of God, that the Son of God may be glorified through it." (Jn 11:4)

When John speaks of the Father glorifying Jesus, he means the Father making his presence in power more manifest in the humanity of Jesus. (The Word has the fullness of God's glory in eternity. In the incarnation we are dealing with the manifestation of this glory in the humanity assumed by the Word.) When he speaks of Jesus glorifying the Father, he means the same thing from Jesus' side: Jesus manifesting more and more the majesty and life of the Father to the world. When John speaks of Jesus glorifying the disciples, he is here referring to the external manifestation of the life of the Father as it is passed on to mankind through the humanity of Jesus.

Before proceeding it would be good briefly to point out a considerable difference in orientation between St.

Paul and St. John in the matter of incarnation and resurrection. In St. Paul's characteristic approach, God's
Son (Paul does not call him the *Word,* although he
does seem to identify the *mystery* the Father reveals
with the Word someway [Col 1:25-26; 4:2]) "humbles"
himself by taking on our mortal flesh as man, and as he
enters more deeply into the limitations of the human
condition, there is a gradual abasement, culminating in
his lowly death. Since his death is the supreme obe-
dience to the Father of Jesus as man, the Father raises
him up in the power of the Spirit. The Spirit suffuses
Christ's humanity, and through it the Spirit is bestowed
on men, giving them solidarity with him and therefore a
share in his victory. In other words, from the moment
of incarnation to the passion and death, there is a
downward movement. The classic statement of Paul on
this theme is the hymn in his Letter to the Philippians:

Though his state was divine,
he did not regard equality with God
as something to cling to,
but emptied himself
to assume the condition of a slave,
being born as men are.
And being found in humble state,
he humbled himself,
becoming obedient unto death,
even death on a cross.

Therefore God highly exalted him,
and bestowed on him
a name above every name,
so that at the name of Jesus
every knee should bend,
in heaven, on earth, and under the earth,
and every tongue proclaim
unto the glory of the Father,
"Jesus Christ is Lord!" (Phil 2:6-11)

St. John's viewpoint, although it can be reconciled with Paul's, is very distinctive. The movement from the incarnation to the crucifixion is all upwards. He sees the Word as entering the human race, and gradually releasing his power and glory into humanity because of the incarnation. One by one the limitations of man are transformed by being caught up in the glory of the Word who has embraced them. Death then becomes the high point, not the low point, since at the moment of death the Word's glory is poured out into this last, most terrible defeat for man, and overpowers it with victory. In John's synthetic vision he does not see death and resurrection so much as separate events, but as one and the same event, victorious death.

Although John gives a role to the Spirit in the question of power over death and of human solidarity with Christ, he also explains this in terms of glory. (On analysis *glory* in John's writings is frequently equivalent to *Spirit* in Paul's.)

We must deal then with two phases of the revelation of glory: that which manifests itself in Jesus in the movement toward his death and resurrection, and the glory as it is communicated to mankind through the glorification of Jesus.

7. The Grain of Wheat

Although it was the Word of God who took our human nature, it does not mean that Jesus was not truly man while still being God. If he were not, our liberation could never have taken place from within, since it is in Jesus' real humanity that we have solidarity with him. To put it in an oversimplified way, because Jesus was man and precisely as man freely accepted his human history unto his death, it is man and man's death that are transformed from within. But because Jesus was not only man but God, the incarnate Word whose power was released into his humanity, that very transformation from within was possible and accomplished.

The New Testament writers were not concerned with the philosophical implications of the incarnation, what it meant in metaphysical terms that Jesus was both God and man. Some measure of clarity in philosophical terms was brought to the matter only throughout centuries of theological reflection in the Church, although even then it remains a mystery beyond our complete grasp.

Yet the data reflected on by theologians are what are found in the New Testament. In John especially many of the elements for subsequent inquiry are vividly discernible. Jesus is God, the incarnate Word, the Son of the Father. He is man, has his own individual human history, dies as a man freely accepting his crucifixion,

and thereby brings about our freedom and victory.
Jesus is one person.

Nowhere in John is the relationship between the
Word and the humanity assumed by the Word more
clearly brought out than in the narratives of the death
and resurrection of Jesus. Were Jesus to have died a
"quiet, natural" death, human death would thereby
surely have been transformed. There would have been
reason enough to appreciate the tension involved: the
glory of the Word who is Life in a victorious conflict
with the powers of death. But the fact is that Jesus, as
every man, had his own concrete history, which for him
involved a dramatic and painful death. All the forces of
evil seem unleashed against Life and there is a clash of
cosmic proportions.

It is as if it were not enough for man to be set free
from death by a simple, rather spontaneous event.
Rather, all that is or can be negative and death-dealing
in man's life had to be marshalled together in force
and in the flesh to oppose and to be overcome by the
glory of the incarnate Word: darkness, sin, voluntary
blindness, hatred, despair. Man seems almost to chal-
lenge God by bringing forth the depths of his misery
and alienation with the taunt: Can you heal *this*?

The magnitude of this confrontation underlines the
nature of Jesus' free decision to accept it as he saw
more and more of the darkness of the powers lining up
against him:

My soul is troubled now. And what shall I say, "Father, save me from this hour"? No, it is for this purpose
that I have come to this hour! Father, glorify your
name! (Jn 12:27-28a) For this my Father loves me, that
I lay down my life that I might take it up again. No
one takes it from me; I lay it down freely. I have power

to lay it down, and I have power to take it up again. This is the mandate I have received from my Father. (Jn 10:17-18)

God so loved the world that he sent his Son to bring it life. That Life, the reality of the Father, would burst forth in glory at the *hour,* the moment when crucifixion and resurrection, death and life, would meet in final and definitive conflict. Jesus as man accepted this mission freely.

Jesus mentions more than once that his glory will be fully manifest only at that hour. When Mary his mother asks him to perform a sign at Cana, therein revealing his glory, he replies, "My hour has not yet come." (Jn 2:4b) Similarly, his companions say to him:

You should leave here and go to Judea, so that your disciples may see the works you're doing. If you want to be known publicly, you shouldn't work in secret. If you're going to perform works like this, display yourself to the world! (Jn 7:3-4)

Jesus answers them, "It is not yet the right time for me. . . . You go up to the festival, but for me, the right time has not fully come." (Jn 7:6a, 8)

Jesus does decide to go up to the feast anyway. On the last day of the festival he stands up and proclaims, "If anyone thirsts, let him come to me. Let him drink, who believes in me. As the Scripture says, 'From within him shall flow rivers of living water.' " (Jn 7:37-39) John explains: "He was here referring to the Spirit, which those who believed in him would receive. The Spirit, of course, had not yet been given, since Jesus was not yet glorified." (Jn 7:39)

The Jews, especially the Pharisees, personify in

John's Gospel the growing forces of opposition to the revelation of Jesus' glory. The more Jesus gradually lets his glory be seen in his signs and works, the more they blind themselves to the *truth* and seek to kill him. They are held in check, however, until the power of darkness may expose itself to the fullest, creating the maximum tension only at the hour where Light and darkness will appear in the strongest contrast. "They tried to seize him to kill him, but no one laid hands on him, since his hour had not yet come." (Jn 7:20)

The rising confrontation between Jesus and those who sought to kill him, as described in Chapters Seven-Eleven of John's Gospel, is charged and dramatic in its crescendo. Jesus tells them they will die in their sins and blindness for rejecting him in unbelief; they say he is mad, possessed, that he must be put to death.

When finally man's despair and self-alienation have marshalled themselves together against the one who would bring light into their darkness, if only they would put aside their blindness, Jesus proclaims to his disciples: "Now has the hour come for the Son of man to be glorified!" (Jn 12:23) The glory will come about through and in death itself, so that man's alienation will be healed from within at its roots: "Unless the grain of wheat falls into the earth and dies, it remains alone. But if it dies, it produces much fruit." (Jn 12:24) Jesus applies this same principle to those who would share in his victory: like him, we must find our resurrection not outside of or in spite of our human condition or suffering, but within it. "He who loves his life destroys it. He who hates his life in this world, preserves it for eternal life. If anyone would serve me, let him follow me. Where I am, there will my servant be." (Jn 12:25-26a)

(It should be noted here that when Jesus speaks of

"going," he means passing through his death to the Father. This constitutes the *exodus* or passover theme which occurs throughout John's Gospel, especially in the Last Supper discourse. We will later expand on this theme when we speak of Jesus as Alpha and Omega.)

Because Jesus' triumph takes place precisely in his death, the very time when the energies of darkness appear to be in ascendency against him, Jesus declares: "Now will the prince of this world be driven out, and when I am lifted up from this earth, I will draw all men to myself." (Jn 12:31) The "prince of this world" is, of course, Satan, personifying all the assembled energies of evil. By Jesus' crucifixion and death, these energies will paradoxically be overcome, and man will be set free from death, drawn through Jesus to the Father. John uses the ambiguous "lifted up" to indicate that for Jesus death and resurrection are the same event: to be crucified is to be exalted.

The Last Supper discourse in John's Gospel is so rich in content and expression that there is the temptation to quote it here almost in full. Some of its themes have already been touched on; others we will pursue in subsequent chapters. The reader is strongly encouraged at this point to set this book aside and to read the discourse through in its entirety.

Let us cite just a few more key passages that bring together the theme of Jesus' glorification in his death. Note especially that Jesus asks explicitly that the glory of the Word, discernible only partly in Jesus before this time, be released into his humanity in its fullness. Observe also that he identifies this release of glory in death as transforming mortal flesh, thereby bringing life to men. Life for men is described in terms we have seen: experiencing the Father in Jesus.

Now is the Son of man glorified, and God is glorified in
him. God will thereby give him glory in himself, and
will give him glory soon. (Jn 13:31-32)

Father, the hour has come! Give glory to your Son,
that your Son may give glory to you—just as you have
given him power over all flesh, to give eternal life to all
whom you have given to him. This is eternal life: that
they know you, the only true God, and Jesus Christ
whom you have sent. I have given you glory on earth by
bringing to completion what you gave me to do. Now,
Father, give me glory in your presence, the glory I had
with you before the world began. (Jn 17:1-5)

Father, I desire that those you have given me may be
with me where I am, that they may see my glory, which
you have given me, out of your love for me, before the
foundation of the world. (Jn 17:24)

The scenes that follow the Last Supper—the arrest in
the garden, the interrogations before Annas and Caia-
phas with Peter's denial of Jesus, the judgment and the
crucifixion—incorporate frequent echoes of the major
Gospel motifs. "Whom do you seek?" Jesus asks the
guards about to arrest him, just as he had asked his first
disciples. "Jesus the Nazorean." "I AM," Jesus answers, and the soldiers fall back in awe. *I AM* is a
divine title, the name Yahweh revealed to Moses. Jesus
tells Pilate he has come into the world to bear witness
to the truth. "What is truth?" Pilate retorts. Given
John's special meaning for this word, his whole Gospel
seems to be written almost as the answer to Pilate's
question.

Finally Jesus is led to crucifixion outside the city
wall. From the cross he entrusts his mother Mary to
John, whom he loved. "Woman, this is your son." (Jn
19:26) The title *woman* evokes the scene with Mary at

Cana, when his "hour had not yet come." (Jn 2:4)

After that, knowing that all was now fulfilled, that Scripture might be completely fulfilled, Jesus said, "I am thirsty." There was a jar there of common wine, so they stuck a sponge soaked in this wine on some hyssop and raised it to his mouth. When Jesus had taken the wine he said, "It is finished." He bowed his head and handed over the spirit." (Jn 19:28-30)

"All is finished"—the Word has entered man's world in the flesh unto death. Symbolically, Jesus thirsts and drinks: "Am I not to drink the cup the Father has given me?" (Jn 18:11) But in this very act of dying, Jesus is victorious and man is freed from death. As he breathes his last, he hands over the Spirit, the promised advocate whose outpouring would be a sign of Jesus' glorification.

Jesus' triumph in death, the hour of his glory, enters into human history with the resurrection of his transformed flesh. Man challenged God with the miseries and darkness of his humanity, and God overwhelmed them with glory in the humanity of his Son. We must remember that the overflowing of the glory of the Father's Word into the body of Jesus opens up for every man access to this glory. When one contemplates the glorification of Jesus in his humanity, then, let him know that although "it does not yet appear what we shall be, we know that when he appears, we shall be like him, for we shall see him as he is." (1 Jn 3:2)

Before Jesus' glorification the believer could be led to experience the presence of the Father in Jesus. After the glorification in the resurrection the experience seems ineluctable. Significantly, even here, John indicates, the experience of the resurrection glory comes through the experience of the cross:

He said to Thomas, "Put your finger here and examine my hands. Put your hand into my side. Do not persist in your unbelief, but believe!" Thomas answered him, "My Lord and my God!" (Jn 20:27-28)

In the Apocalypse Jesus who "died and lives forever" (Apoc 1:18) is simultaneously the glorified paschal lamb and the wounded lamb. The act of triumph in defeat becomes an eternal moment where death meets life. (It might be observed here that in the Christian Eucharistic liturgy the paschal mystery is not repeated. Rather through the sacramental activity of the Church, there is a continually renewed access to this one everlasting event.)

8. The Spirit of Truth

The question we posed at the outset was: How do we find access to God the Father, the source and end of our being? The answer we gave was that Jesus is the way to the Father; in him God is made manifest and accessible: "He who sees me sees the Father." This urged the further question: We do not see Jesus. How do we find access to *him*? Unlike Nicodemus, Philip and the woman at the well, we are not present to him face to face. He is risen and returned to the Father.

We are now in a position to pursue this second question more directly. The general framework of our reflections will be this: The Father sends the Son to us, and through the Son, the Spirit. The Spirit is released in power upon man through the humanity of Jesus in the passion-resurrection event. Or, in more Johannine terms, the glory the Word had from the beginning with the Father is fully manifested in the humanity the Word assumes, and man partakes of this glory. Jesus returns to the Father in glory, man in solidarity with him. The paschal event is the center of the divine sending and returning, the point at which we are caught up in the process.

I came from the Father and have come into the world. Again, I leave the world and go to the Father. . . . The Father will send the Spirit in my name. You know him, because he remains with you and will be within you. . . . In my Father's house are many rooms; were it not so, would I have told you that I was going to prepare a place for you? I am indeed going to prepare a place for you, and then I shall return and take you to myself, that where I am, you may be . . . that [you] may see the glory which [the Father] has given me before the foundation of the world. (Jn 16:28; 14:16-17; 26:1-3; 17:24).

It might be visualized this way:

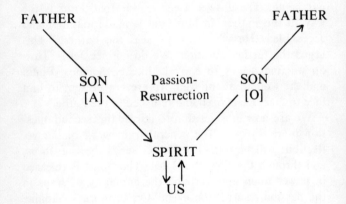

Or, from another perspective:

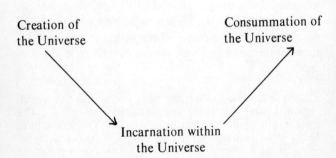

There is thus a great sweep of love *from* the Father through Christ in the Spirit, *to* the Father through Christ in the Spirit. The Son sent and the Son returning are, of course, one and the same person. For us, however, there is definitely a difference of aspect. The first is the Son sent by the Father, bringing the Father to us. In him the universe is created. The second is the Son returning to the Father, bringing us to the Father. In him the universe is consummated. When we speak of this later, we will use the expression of the Apocalypse and refer to Jesus as both Alpha and Omega, the Beginning and the End.

Let us consider first of all the transformation of the disciples in the paschal event when the Spirit and the glory are released into the humanity of Jesus. There is a series of statements by Christ when he is speaking about the meaning of the paschal mystery in the form "As the Father . . . so the Son . . . and so now you," or "As I . . . so you." They indicate that in the passion-resurrection, the reality that Jesus embodies as the incarnate Word of the Father is in some measure passed on to the disciples. The movement is as in our diagram: not from the Father to the Son to us and then back to Jesus as "Alpha," but from the Father to the Son to us *out to other people through human history,* and only through human history returning back to Jesus as "Omega," the consummator of the universe. The dynamism of the sweep is the activity of the Spirit.

Most striking of these statements is Jesus' commandment of love:

As the Father has loved me, so I have loved you. Live on in my love. If you keep my commandments, you will live on in my love, just as I have kept the Father's commandments and live on in his love . . . This is my commandment, that you love one another as I have loved you. (Jn 15:9-12, 15)

Earlier he had said, "If you love me, keep my commandments." (Jn 14:15) This would seem to imply that we return to Jesus who approaches us. But no, his commandment is precisely that we enter history: "Love one another." Jesus indicates that it is this love that will eventually join us to him again at the end of our history. His commandment to love is given in the context of explaining that he is going away and for a time they will not see him, but later they would see him. *The bridge between seeing him now and seeing him then is their love for one another.* Here there is an interplay between the Father's love being poured out for them through Christ in the Spirit at the resurrection and our love in the Spirit leading us back through Christ to the Father.

The eschatology or description of the return to the Father is not so explicitly worked out in John's First Letter, but the same thought is there:

Beloved, let us love one another, because love is of God, and he who loves is born of God and knows God. The man who does not love does not know God, because God is love. God's love was made manifest in us in this, that God sent his only Son into the world that we might have life through him. Love then is this, not that we have loved God, but that he has loved us, and sent his Son as an expiation for our sins. Beloved, if God has so loved us, we must also then love one another. No one has ever seen God, but *if we love one another, God dwells in us and his love is brought to perfection in us.* (1 Jn 4:7-12)

This process happens in the Spirit: "The way we know

we remain in God and he in us is that he has given us of his Spirit." (1 Jn 4:13) The love we have for one another leads us back through Christ to the Father: "See what love the Father has given us in letting us be called his children! What we shall later be is not yet clear, but we know that when he comes we shall be like him, because we shall see him as he is!" (1 Jn 3:1-2)

These are the elements that emerge from the commandment of love: (1) There is an outpouring from the Father through Jesus to us in the Spirit. (2) In the paschal mystery we begin to partake of this outpouring, we actually share in the reality of the Father in a way parallel to Jesus' embodiment of this reality. (3) We thereby become, just as Jesus was, the experience of God for one another—this, if we exercise such a prerogative by loving. "I solemnly tell you, he who receives anyone I send, receives me, and he who receives me receives him who sent me." (Jn 13:20) (4) Through entering into love for one another, that is, by entering into our human history toward the future, we return in the Spirit through Jesus to the Father.

Where, then, do we find access to Jesus who is access to the Father? In one another, in the Christian community, and especially, we shall see, when that community collectively brings its God-given life to bear on its members in what we call its sacramental activity.

Let us examine these elements as they are found in a few other similarly structured passages of John's Gospel and First Letter. The "grain of wheat" passage, to which we have already made reference, should take on new meaning in the present context. Jesus is about to undergo his passion and death, and from the midst of this his glory will burst forth: "Now has the hour come for the Son of man to be glorified. Unless the grain of wheat falls into the earth and dies, it remains alone. But it if dies, it produces much fruit." Jesus then indicates that just as he returns to the Father in glory by entering fully into his humanity unto death, so man must try to find his transcendence and liberation not by bracketing his suffering and by sidestepping the involvement in and demands of his history and the human condition, but only by entering into them as Jesus did. In this way he will find resurrection from within (because of what Jesus did to human history *from within*), and be led to the Father in Jesus. "Loving your life" in this context means seeking your fulfillment as a direct end of your endeavors; "hating your life" means finding your fulfillment in the emptying-out love for others such as Jesus manifested in his passion.

He who loves his life destroys it; he who hates his life in this world, keeps it for eternal life. If anyone would serve me, let him follow me. Where I am, there will my servant be. If anyone serves me, the Father will honor him. (Jn 12:25-26)

A similar theme is explicitated in Jesus' explanation of his washing the feet of the disciples. Again, as Jesus has done, so must they do. They must find their transcendence in service: "I have given you an example, so that you might also do what I have done for you. A servant is not greater than his master." (Jn 13:15-16a)

It is not just a question of the disciples following Jesus' example as a sort of imitative or parallel activity. The very reality which was in Jesus and which manifested itself in power at the passion-resurrection takes hold of the disciples from within and becomes the new inner basis of their operations. If their activity is now to be like Jesus', it is because they themselves are like

Jesus: "As he is, so are we in the world." (1 Jn 4:17b)

Jesus sometimes calls this inner actuality the Father dwelling in the disciples, sometimes himself dwelling in them, and sometimes the Spirit. He also calls it their glorification. It is accomplished, he says, by the glory which he had from the beginning as the eternal Word being released in him at the *hour* and being given to the disciples, or by his going to the Father whence he will send the Spirit to them. Really these both are the same paschal event, described alternately from the aspect of coming to it or returning from it. Therefore the new presence in the disciples is not a static thing, but involves by its very nature an "exodus," an assimilation into the coming and returning of Jesus.

I solemnly tell you, he who believes in me will do the works that I do, and far greater than these he shall do, because I go to the Father. . . . In a little while the world will see me no more. But you will see me, because I live and you will live. On that day you will know that I am in my Father and you in me and I in you. . . . If anyone loves me, he will keep my word, and my Father will love him, and we will come to him and make our home with him. (Jn 14:12, 19b-20, 23)

It is the function of the Spirit to join us to Christ and therefore to the Father. The Spirit establishes the relationship both retrospectively and prospectively: he proceeds from the Father through the Son-as-Alpha to us in Christ's glory, constitutes the milieu of our present participation in liberation and transcendence, and brings us back to and through Christ-as-Omega in his return to the Father.

I have told you these things while I am still with you. But the Paraclete, the Holy Spirit, whom the Father

will send in my name, he will teach you everything and
bring to your remembrance all that I have told you.
. . . When the Paraclete comes, whom I shall send to
you from the Father, the Spirit of *truth* who proceeds
from the Father, he will bear witness to me. You also
are witnesses, because you have been with me from the
beginning. . . . When the Spirit of truth comes, he will
guide you on the way to all *truth*. He will not speak on
his own, but will speak what he hears, and will an-
nounce to you the things that are to come. He will glorify me, because he will take what is mine and declare it
to you. All the Father has is mine. That is why I said
he will take what is mine and declare it to you. (Jn
14:25-26; 15:26-27; 16:13-15)

Recall John's use of *truth* as the experience of the
Father in Jesus. The Spirit, as the Spirit of truth, brings
about the experience of the Father in Jesus into our
midst. That is why he is said to "bring to our remembrance" all that Jesus told us. He makes Jesus present
to us, even within us, and through Jesus, the reality of
the Father. Note how the Spirit leads us to Christ-as-
Omega, reaching out from Christ at the end of our history to us, pulling us into the future: "He will 'declare'
to you the things that are to come."

Christ's glory is closely identified with the Spirit,
since the Spirit is the presence of God in power. The
Spirit is the loving union between the Father and the
Son, between the Father, the Son and us, and between
us and one another, as we are caught up into their activity.

I do not pray for these only, but also for those who
believe in me because of their word, so that they may
all be one, as you, Father, are in me and I in you—that
they may also be in us, that the world may believe that
you sent me. The glory that you have given me I have

given to them, so that they may be one just as we are one—I in them and you in me, that they may be perfectly one, so that the world may know that you have sent me, and have loved them just as you have loved me. Father, I desire that those you have given me may be with me where I am, that they may see my glory which you have given me out of your love for me, before the foundation of the world. Just Father, although the world has not known you, I have known you, and these know that you have sent me. I have made your name known to them and will make it known, so that the love with which you have loved me may be in them, and I in them. (Jn 17:20-26)

Finally, then, the Spirit brings about the penetration of the incarnation of the Word into space and time, to be consummated only at the end of human history when all is returned to the Father in Christ, as St. Paul puts it: "Each in his own order: Christ the first fruits, then, at his coming, all who belong to Christ. Then comes the end, when he will hand over the kingdom to God the Father." (1 Cor 15:23-24a) In John:

I solemnly tell you, you will weep and mourn while the world rejoices. You will be sorrowful, but your sorrow will be turned to joy. When a woman is in childbirth, she is in pain because her hour approaches. But when she has delivered her child, she no longer remembers her suffering, for joy that a man has been brought into the world." (Jn 16:20-21)

Yes, the pain of childbirth, the grain of wheat falling into the ground so that it may bear much fruit, the branches, attached to Christ the vine, which must be pruned to be productive. Because we are assimilated to Christ in the Spirit. our return to the Father through Christ will be as his return, through our history and humanity, not outside of them.

If the world hates you, know that it has hated me before it has hated you. . . . Remember the word I have spoken to you: a servant is not above his master. If they kept my word, they will keep yours also. (Jn 15:18, 20)

In a word, "I no longer call you servants, but friends . . . for a servant does not know what his master is doing. No, I call you friends because I have made known to you all I have heard from the Father." (Jn 15:15) And the consequential ongoing dynamic of this new relationship and profound inner reality: "This I command you, love one another." (Jn 15:17)

9. Love One Another

Let us tie together much of what we have been describing, especially in the last chapter, with what John has to say about *love*. John uses the word *love* well over a hundred times in his writings.

When we spoke about *word* and *truth,* we said that these Johannine words indicated various aspects of Jesus' embodying the reality of the Father. This reality is love. John uses *love* in analogous ways, but the prime referent is God himself, the Father, whose very existence is the activity of love: "God *is* love, and he who abides in love abides in God, and God abides in him." (1 Jn 4:16b) Or again, "He who does not love does not know God, because God is love." (1 Jn 4:8)

Since God is love, every activity that flows from God is an act of love. What is more, wherever it manifests itself, love is ultimately attributable to God, whether because it proceeds directly and personally from him, or because when someone else loves, he is entering into God's own activity and sharing in it.

Beloved, let us love one another, because love is of God, and he who loves is born of God and knows God. . . . Love consists in this, not that we have loved God, but that he has loved us. (1 Jn 4:7, 10a)

The Word is the external manifestation of the Father, and Jesus is the Word made flesh—the reality of the Father made accessible. John had called this reality

65

made accessible in Jesus *life,* but now we see that the life of God is nothing other than love. John says indirectly several times that in sending his Son, the Word, Jesus, to us, he is sending love to us.

God's love was made manifest to us in this way, that he sent his only Son into the world, that we might have life through him. Love consists in this, not that we have loved God, but that he has loved us and has sent his Son to be the expiation of our sins. . . . God so loved the world that he gave his only Son, that whoever believes in him should not perish, but have everlasting life. (1 Jn 4:9-10; Jn 3:16)

Note how in these passages John stresses that Jesus is the revelation of God's love *to us, for us.* In the incarnation the Word is spoken *to us:* it is meant to let the reality of God, love, burst forth on our horizon and enter into our lives: "As the Father has loved me, I have loved you. Remain on in my love." (Jn 15:9)

[Father], I have revealed your name to them, and I will continue to reveal it, so that the love with which you have loved me may be in them, and that I may be in them . . . so that the world may know that you have sent me and have loved them as you have loved me. (Jn 17:26, 23b)

When individuals encounter Jesus during his ministry, it is clear that love is coextensive with their belief in him. John characterizes belief in Jesus as acknowledging him as coming from the Father. Since the Father is love, and Jesus is, therefore, incarnate love, one cannot believe in Jesus as coming from the Father if he has cut himself off from love.

You do not have the Father's word abiding in you,

because you do not believe him whom he has sent. . . .
You refuse to come to me that you may have life. . . .
I know that God's love is not in you. I have come in my
Father's name, and yet you do not accept me. (Jn 5:38,
40, 42-43a)

If God were your Father, you would love me, because I
proceeded and have come forth from God. I came not
on my own, but he sent me. Why do you not understand what I say? Because you cannot bear to hear my
word. . . . He who is of God hears the words of God;
you do not hear them because you are not of God. (Jn
8:42-43, 47)

They do not hear because they are "not of God." How
is that? "Love is of God. He who loves is born of God
and knows God. He who does not love does not know
God, for God is love." (1 Jn 4:7b-8)

Strictly speaking it is in the passion, death, resurrection and the sending of the Spirit by Jesus (all of which
constitute for John a single paschal event), where the
transformation of the disciples in Jesus' love takes
place. In Jesus' triumph over death the disciples receive
the Spirit whose dynamism inserts them into Jesus' return to the Father in glory. The disciples are told to
love not just in imitation of Christ's love, but because
they are now animated by the same principle of operation which is Jesus'. It was the inner actuality we spoke
of in the last chapter, which John alternately called
glory, the indwelling of the Father and himself, or the
presence of the Spirit.

This event, when the disciple comes to share in
Christ's transcendent power, is frequently called a *being
born* or a *rebirth,* and by it one becomes a *child of God.*
"See what love the Father has given us that we should
be called God's children! Yet that is what we are!" (1

Jn 3:1a) By such a rebirth one no longer lives with just
his own power of life, but with the life which is God's,
the life that is love. Indeed, to love as one has been
loved by God is the very sign that one has been reborn:

This is how all men will know that you are my disciples, that you have love for one another. (Jn 13:55)

This is how to tell who are the children of God and who
are the children of the devil: whoever does not do right
is not of God, nor he who does not love his brother.
. . . We know we have passed from death to life in that
we love the brethren. He who does not love is still in
death. . . . We love because he first loved us. (1 Jn
3:10, 14; 4:19)

Love is not a commodity which one can hold on to as
a possession. It is an activity, a motion. Hence the person who experiences the love of God for himself passes
on that love to his brothers. "As I have loved you, so
love one another." (Jn 15:12) One does, of course, love
God in return, but precisely *in returning,* in going back
to God through our history as it is realized in and
through our love for one another. "This is the commandment we have from him, that the one who loves
God love also his brother." (1 Jn 4:21)

To repeat what we have said before, one does not return to Jesus as Alpha, the Jesus who came as God's
love to us. One returns to Jesus as Omega, going to the
Father, awaiting us at the end of our human enterprise,
whom we approach by entering into our history
through love, as he did.

No one has ever seen God. But if we love one another,
God lives in us, and his love is brought to completion in
us. . . . For he who does not love his brother whom he
sees, cannot love God whom he has not seen. . . . Love

is brought to completion in us that we have confidence for the day of judgment. (1 Jn 4:12, 20b, 17)

Love is our bond with the future where Christ awaits us, "when we shall be like him and see him as he is." (1 Jn 3:2) It is a real bond, since it flows from the presence of the Spirit who is our existential nexus to Jesus:

God is love, and he who abides in love abides in God, and God abides in him. . . . And this is how we know we abide in him and he in us, because he has given us of his Spirit. (1 Jn 4:16b, 13)

Love, then, is a "hot potato." We cannot grasp it and hold on to it, we must give it to another. If one refuses to love another, he is breaking the motion that began with God's love for him and which must be passed on to be viable. "If a man has the world's goods and sees his brother in need, yet closes his heart to him, how does God's love abide in him?" (1 Jn 3:17) And "we know we have passed out of death into life because we love our brothers. Anyone who does not love remains in death." (1 Jn 3:14) In a real sense, if one refuses to love, that is, refuses to carry God's love for him into the future by his love for others, he thereby effectively denies this love given to him in the past: "Whoever does not love his brother is not from out of God." (1 Jn 3:10b)

Conversely, to affirm love as our activity reaching into the future is to affirm God's antecedent love for us. In a word, to love is to accept love, to accept love is to love. In a real way we make our past to be by what we make our future to be. Although John says that *love is* because God first loved us, he also implies that our loving allows God's love *to be for us:* "He who loves has been born of God." (1 Jn 4:7b)

Love paradoxically drives us into human history with its limitations, and at the same time transcends human history and liberates us from its limitations. It drives us into history because love means being united with Jesus' glorious return to the Father which was achieved by entering fully into the human situation in the incarnation, even unto death. Jesus was the "grain of wheat" (Jn 12:23-26) which had to fall into the ground to produce life, and if we are to be where he is, we must follow him. "As he is, so are we in the world." (1 Jn 4:17b)

Love will not allow us to be closed up within ourselves, withdrawn from people and the world, holding on to God's love for us while we await the end. It is only by going out in love that God's love abides in us. Not just *going out* in love, but by *emptying ourselves out* in love as Jesus did—not seeking our own security by pulling in and consolidating, but by giving. "He who loves his life destroys it; he who hates his life in this world keeps it for eternal life." (Jn 12:25)

This willingness to empty ourselves out in love must be total, as was Jesus' willingness. How our love will in fact be realized in our history we do not know— "What concern is that of yours? Follow me!" (Jn 21:22b)—but we must be open to the possibilities, knowing that despite our fears we have Jesus' own power to love given to us. "Perfect love casts out fear." (1 Jn 4:18)

Thus, because Jesus died for us, explaining that "No man has greater love than this, that he lay down his life for his friends," (Jn 13:13) John does not hesitate to say, "We came to know love because he laid down his life for us; we too must lay down our lives for our brothers." (1 Jn 3:16) The ironic thing is that there are probably many among us who might, in our imagination, be willing to lay down our lives for our brothers or to perform some other heroic deed of such caliber. That is true probably because such acts, especially if public, are dramatic—we picture ourselves as so many Sydney Cartons making the ultimate sacrifice for Charles Darnay—and in a sense have their own reward. Sometimes we would prefer the scourge of a persecutor with all the sympathy and attention that might draw, to a persistent headache which no one appreciates.

But if we must be willing to die for one another, it stands to reason that we must be willing in love to do anything short of that, and this includes the ordinary, everyday, undramatic marks of love—patient endurance, a willingness to listen, little generosities, trust in spite of evidence to the contrary, doing the unpleasant for the unpleasant, and the myriad other things that characterize most of our human dealings with one another. How often have we met people who are anxious to expend their energies and lives for some great social or charitable cause and who wouldn't give you the time of day! "Little children, let us love in deed and in truth, not just in word!" (1 Jn 3:18)

If love plunges us into history, it also enables us to transcend history, to soar beyond the limitations of space and time. This is true, of course, because Christian love is rooted in the death and resurrection of Jesus, that single event where man's greatest apparent defeat becomes his greatest victory, where the most binding of man's chains are loosed by the limitlessness of God in Jesus.

To love, after all, is to share in the life of God which knows no limit. Compared with it, man's confined life without God is viewed as a sort of death: "We know that we have passed out of death into life because we love our brothers." (1 Jn 3:14a) The Father has life in himself, the Word embodies it in the incarnation, and those who believe in Jesus share in this life, which is the activity of love. To give this life is Jesus' constant promise.

John consistently calls God's life in which we share *eternal life*. Although *eternal* includes a temporal meaning for John, that is, it says that life never ends—sometimes he says specifically *everlasting life*—it means much more than that. Since it is the life of God who pre-exists creation and who is independent of and not limited by it, it is a life that is not tied down to duration, space, boundaries. It is transcendent, unlimited life, not just quantitatively, but qualitatively different from man's. This life enters time and space through Jesus' incarnation, and if we are branches on Jesus, the vine, we have a share in it. So different is this life that, as we have said, a man who enters into it is said to be reborn. "Beloved, we are *God's* children now!" (1 Jn 3:2a)

God is life. God is love. Since to be or to live for God is to love, love then, when we have God's life within us, makes it possible to break out of our confinement and to leap beyond our historical categories of boundaries. The love with which we love is from the eternal and limitless God. The ultimate object of our love as we exercise it for our brothers is again God himself, waiting for us at the consummation of the universe as we approach him through Christ in the Spirit. In one sense we are with God now, because we share his life and, as John says, we "know" him. In another sense we long for God, because we as yet encounter him as grains of wheat in the earth, that is, in the human situation, and we wait for the incarnation and glorification to have their final effect in our universe when Jesus presents us definitively to the Father. We are in process, in union through the Spirit with our goal, but we are not yet at rest in it. "Beloved, we are God's children *now,* but it is not yet clear what we shall be. We do know, though, that when he appears we shall be like him because we will see him as he is." (1 Jn 3:2)

We can see some of the transcendent and boundary-straining qualities of our love in our own experience. Above all, love not only says "I am for you now," it also says "I will be for you in the future, no matter what happens." Love that is conditional is really not love. Love is faithful and long-suffering, because it hopes for its final fulfillment in Christ. Fidelity is *the* mark of love's transcendence, the quality that enables our love to break through the here and now. Love is then a commitment to the future *to be for someone,* and thus is an act of supreme freedom that goes beyond dimensions. It *must* have this futurewards fidelity and pledge of constancy, since it is our link with Christ as Omega at the end of time. Just as Jesus is the Word of love spoken to man, the Word which must go forth and not return empty to the Father, so our love, once uttered in our history, must never return empty, but go forward until it rests with the Father in Christ. "Love is brought to completion in us that we may have confidence for the day of judgment." (1 Jn 4:17)

Since God is love, "he who loves *knows* God." (1 Jn 4:7b) John, recall, uses *know* with the sense of interpersonal encounter. The dynamic is this: when we love, we do so not with our own native power, but with the communicated activity of God, who by our loving dwells in us through Jesus in the Spirit.

[Father], the love with which you loved me will be in them, and I in them. . . . If a man loves me, he will keep my word, and my Father will love him, and we will come and make our home within him. (Jn 17:26b, 14:23) [To love Jesus is to keep his commandments. (Jn 14:21) His commandment is to love one another. (Jn 15:9-12)]

In love we know God "through a glass darkly," as Paul says, and not yet face-to-face. Yet, although the process has not yet reached its fulfillment, it is genuinely God whom we encounter in love. It is analogous to seeing the Father in the incarnate Word: "Philip, he who sees me is actually seeing the Father." (Jn 14:9b)

Jesus referred to the possibility of experiencing the Father in himself as *truth*. (See Chapter Four.) Similarly, love and truth are associated in John's writings.

The elder to the elect lady [i.e., some particular church] and her children whom I love in the truth—and not only I, but also all those who have come to know the truth, because of the truth that abides in us and will be with us forever. May grace, mercy and peace be with us from God the Father and from Jesus Christ, the Father's Son, in truth and love. (2 Jn 1-3)

If one does not love, he does not have the truth, that is, the experience of God is closed to him. He is said to walk in the darkness, because he is blinded and cannot "see":

Beloved, it is no new commandment which I write to you, but an old one which you had from the beginning, the word you have already heard. Really though, it is a new commandment, which is true in him and in you, because the darkness is passing away and the true light is already shining. Whoever says he is in the light and hates his brother is still in the darkness. It is he who loves his brother that is in the light, and in it there is no cause to stumble. But the man who hates his brother is in the darkness and walks in darkness, not knowing where he is going, because the darkness has blinded his eyes. (1 Jn 2:7-11)

10. Church and Sacrament

Love presupposes community, since love is an outgoing activity which embraces others in unity, with a mutual communication, giving, sharing and deepening of the experience of God. We have seen (Chapter Eight) how Jesus founded a community in the paschal mystery with his glorification and gift of the Spirit, giving them the commandment to love with his love. This community becomes the focal point of Christ's continued presence in man's history, until that history is consummated and returned to the Father in Jesus. The community, which the New Testament, especially in the Letters of Paul, calls the *Church,* begins with Jesus' immediate disciples, but reaches out geographically and in time, assimilating others to itself in belief and the unity of love.

I do not pray for these only, but also for those who believe in me because of their word, so that they may all be one, as you, Father, are in me and I in you—that they may also be in us, that the world may believe that you sent me. [*Note:* the world will know that "Jesus has come" in the love and unity of his disciples!] The glory that you have given me I have given to them, so that they may be one just as we are one—I in them and you in me, that they may be perfectly one, so that the world may know that you have sent me, and have loved them just as you have loved me. . . . I have made your name known to them and will continue to make it known, so that the love with which you have loved me may be in them, and I in them. (Jn 17:20-23, 27)

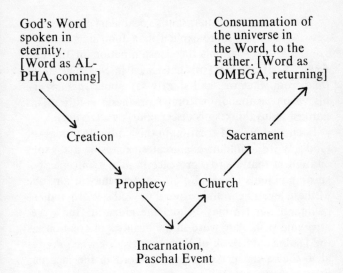

God's Word spoken in eternity. [Word as ALPHA, coming]

Consummation of the universe in the Word, to the Father. [Word as OMEGA, returning]

Creation

Sacrament

Prophecy   Church

Incarnation,
Paschal Event

We call the Church the "focal point" of Christ's continued presence in man's history: "I will be with them." Because God became man, there is no question that all of the human race is changed and caught up in a new direction and reality: "And I, when I am lifted up from the earth, will draw all men to myself." (Jn 12:32) But just as the Word taking flesh marks a further step beyond creation in the explicitation of God's Word in the universe (see Chapter Three), so the Church extends, deepens and spells out the incarnation in man's world. (For this reason Paul calls the Church the "*body* of Christ.") This process peaks in what we call the Church's "sacramental word," when the Church brings its Christ-presence to bear in power on its members, and it is complete at the consummation of the universe in Christ, the final unfolding of God's spoken word, toward which the sacraments have their thrust.

There is no doubt that Paul's vocabulary for this process is richer and more explicit than John's, as is Paul's
vocabulary concerning the consummation of the universe. Yet from what we have seen in St. John so far
(and from what we shall shortly say about *sacrament*),
his vision profoundly encompasses these realities. This
pattern in his thinking is discernible (*see diagram*).

Each step beyond creation in this unilinear process of
God's Word unfolding is a greater expansion and explicitation of that Word's presence in man's universe, be-
speaking God's love and glory. A man may at any one
of these levels hear and respond to God's Word and encounter God. He may behold the glory of God's creative and sustaining word in the beauties of creation, as
the Psalms and Book of Wisdom urged. Or he may realize the saving presence of the Word in the incarnation, as Jesus led Philip to do. He may experience the
manifestation of God in others' love for him, especially
if he makes that love his own interior reality by loving
others himself. Finally, he may be initiated into the ongoing expression and incarnation of God's Word of
love in the community, the church, and its sacramental
activity. [It has become *de rigueur* these days to ex-
coriate the Christian community for its lack of love and
unity, and it is true—insofar as it falls short of love and
unity it falls short of Christ's mandate to it and fails to
manifest his presence. But we musn't be *too* impatient
with the human condition and the dynamics of incarnation.]

Bear in mind what we have said on this matter in an
earlier chapter, how one may distinguish two aspects of
the Word's unfolding as it relates to man. The Word is
Alpha when seen as coming, bringing the Father to us,
and as Omega, when seen as returning, bringing us to

the Father. Strictly speaking, the Passion-Resurrection-Giving of the Spirit is the turning point between coming and returning, but there is a sense in which an individual may be caught up in the process at any step, since even the coming has its finality in the definitive return to the Father and is part of the same motion. It can be said, however, that a man has not received the full impetus of the power that flows from the revelation of the Word until he has encountered it at the level of the paschal event (which is embodied in the Church founded in that event), nor until this point has he been caught up in the full impetus of the return.

At any rate, after the resurrection the Church becomes access to Jesus, the incarnate Word, who is access to the Father. It is by fellowship in the Christian community of love that we have fellowship with the Father in Jesus: "What we have heard—the Word of Life —we proclaim to you so that you may have fellowship with us. Our fellowship is with the Father and with his Son Jesus Christ." (1 Jn 1:[1b], 3)

Jesus' incarnation, passion, resurrection and sending of the Spirit were for all men: "Jesus Christ is an offering for our sins, and not for our sins only, but for those of the whole world." (1 Jn 2:2) As the Church is engaged in its pilgrimage back to the Father through Jesus in the power of the Spirit, all men are called to join the pilgrimage, to encounter Jesus in the Christian community, insofar as it is possible for them to "hear" the word at this level:

I have other sheep who do not belong to this fold. I must lead them also, and they will heed my voice—so that there will be one flock, one shepherd. (Jn 10:16)

Jesus was to die for the nation, and not only for the na-

tion, but to gather into one the dispersed children of
God. (Jn 11:51b-52)

Perhaps there has been no more greatly disputed
aspect of Johannine theology than John's "sacramentalism." There have been some scholars who have
found references to specific sacraments on almost every
page of John. Others deny *any* explicit sacramental references. Although most contemporary exegetes would
admit that at least a few Johannine passages allude to
the sacraments of Baptism and/or the Eucharist [best
candidates in the Gospel are Jn 3:1-8 (Baptism), 4:7-15
(Baptism), 7:37-39 (Baptism), 9:1ff. (Baptism), 13:1ff.
(Baptism), 2:1-11 (Eucharist), 6:1-65 (Eucharist), 15:1-7
(Eucharist), 19:34 and 1 Jn 5:8 (Eucharist and Baptism)], they would deny that any other specific sacraments are alluded to, with the possible exception of Jn
20:23 (Penance), which passage, however, can be in-
terpreted in a much broader sense.

These statistics are not surprising. Although Baptism
and the Eucharist were explicitated by Christ himself
and are clearly in the Church as such from its beginning, founded in the paschal mystery, the Church only
gradually came to distinguish the various other discreet
moments of its sacramental activity. Indeed, this is how
the sacraments should be viewed: not so much as different "acts" of the Church (traditionally seven), but as
an ongoing activity of the Church which "peaks" in
certain specific functions, such as in formally initiating
and incorporating members into itself through Baptism,
or in bringing about the unity of its members with the
Eucharistic presence of its Lord.

It is this level of sacramentalism which is clearest in
John, that is, in seeing the sacraments as one fun-

damental activity of the Christian community wherein it brings the power of Christ to bear on its members, extending the incarnation of the Word into man's history. It might be said that what *signs* (see Chapter Four) were to Jesus in revealing the presence of God, sacramental moments are to the Church in revealing the presence of Jesus.

The *signs* and *works* of Jesus in John's Gospel are deeds, usually miraculous or wonderful, which reveal who Jesus is, the incarnate Word of God, largely through their symbolic nature. We mentioned earlier how Jesus' cure of the man born blind manifested the power of God in Jesus, and through the symbolism of the cure specified that he is the giver of Light to men, the Truth in whom one may find God. His cure of the man on the Sabbath revealed him as Life and the giver of Life:

The Father loves the Son, and shows him everything he is doing. And he will show him even greater works than these, that you may marvel. Just as the Father raises the dead and gives life, so also the Son gives life to whom he wills. (Jn 5:20-21)

In these signs there is a synergy between Jesus' spoken word and some action or use of a material thing. Jesus cures blindness by anointing the eyes with clay and saying, "Go, wash!" (Jn 9:6-7) He changes water into wine, telling the steward to fill the jars and draw from them. This interplay constitutes one symbolic act of power, attesting to the presence of God in Jesus, verified in the result. Before curing the man born blind, Jesus explains that his blindness will let God's works be revealed in him through the cure: "We must do the works of him who sent me while it is day. . . . While I am in the world, I am the light of the world." (Jn 9:4a, 5)

In a sense two levels of God's glory meet in a mutual manifestation: there is Jesus' spoken word, itself an explicitation of Jesus' inner glory, which evokes from creation a marvel and specifies its deeper meaning, and the thing or action, which at Jesus' word is allowed to burst forth from within in a demonstration of God's glory abiding in creation: "The heavens declare the glory of God and the firmament proclaims his handiwork." (Ps 19:2) This relationship between word and action/thing seems to be at the base of Jesus' statement:

Do you not believe that I am in the Father and the Father in me? The words that I say to you I do not speak on my own. The Father who dwells in me is accomplishing his own works. Believe me that I am in the Father and the Father in me. Or else, believe because of the works I do. (Jn 14:10-11)

Just as the Father's presence was made manifest in Jesus through Jesus' word-action signs in which the Father himself worked and was glorified, so in the paschal event Jesus promised to abide in the disciples, thereby enabling them through the power of the Spirit to perform word-action signs which would manifest his presence in them and would glorify him, and through him the Father.

He who believes in me will also do the works I do, and works far greater than these, because I am going to the Father. I will do whatever you ask for in my name, so that the Father may be glorified in the Son. (Jn 14:12-13) [*Note:* the Father will be glorified in the Son by the Son working in the disciples.]

The Spirit will glorify me, because he will take what is mine and declare it to you. All the Father has is mine. That is why I said he will take what is mine and declare it to you. . . . You know the Spirit, because he dwells within you and will be with you. (Jn 16:14-15; 14:17b)

[Father], I have manifested your name to these men whom you have given me out of the world. They were yours, and you gave them to me, and they have kept your word. Now they have come to know that everything you have given me is from you, because the words you gave me I gave them. They have received them and know in truth that I came from you. . . . These men are yours. What is mine is yours, what is yours is mine, and I am glorified in them. I am now no longer in the world, but they are in the world and I am coming to you. . . . I have given them your word. . . . Sanctify them in the truth. Your word is truth. [*Note:* recall the special meaning of *truth* in John.] As you sent me into the world, so I have sent them into the world. And for their sake I consecrate myself, that they also may be consecrated in truth. (Jn 17:6-8a, 9c-11a, 14a, 17-19)

I do not pray for these only, but also for those who believe in me because of their word, so that they may all be one, as you, Father, are in me and I in you—that they may also be in us, that the world may believe that you sent me. [*Note:* the world will know that Jesus is of the Father in knowing that the disciples are of Jesus.] The glory that you have given me I have given to them. . . . I have made your name known to them and will make it known, so that the love with which you have loved me may be in them, and I in them. (Jn 17:20-22a, 26)

When Jesus described the disciples' relationship to him as the branches on the vine, he added: "In this will my Father be glorified, that you bear much fruit, and become my disciples." (Jn 15:8) He repeats this and says immediately, "This I command you, love one another." Love becomes the primal sign or sacrament of the Church, revealing the presence of Jesus working in its midst. Other specifications of the sacramental activity of the Church are judging and reconciling, giving life (i.e., bringing into communion with and sharing in God's life), healing and bringing peace, and establishing a unity of love.

This activity of Jesus, now made the Church's own through its words and actions, is invariably linked with the power of Jesus' Spirit, given to the Church in Jesus' returning to the Father.

As we have mentioned before, the Church has come to regard certain moments in this activity as more essential and characteristic works of bringing its inner power to bear on its members, and has historically called them *sacraments*. The basic sacramental activity of the Church, however, which pervades each of these special moments, remains love.

The most intense of these moments of the Church is the Eucharist, wherein Christ is present not only in the activity of the Church's word, but actually becomes present in the created matter, bread and wine, over which the word is spoken. Here, it would seem, Christ is not "imposed" on these elements from without, but rather the creative Word of the Father present in creation is allowed to explode forth in a way that approaches the incarnation itself. If exegetes are correct in seeing Eucharistic allusions in the vine and branches metaphor, the context implies that the function of this very dramatic presence of Christ in his Church is to bring about love and unity. Above all, this sacrament confers a greater participation in Life, and propels the Christian community forward to its consummation on the last day. In a passage clearly referring to the Christian Eucharist, Jesus proclaims:

He who eats my flesh and drinks my blood has eternal life, and I will raise him up on the last day. My flesh is food indeed, and my blood is drink indeed. He who eats my flesh and drinks my blood abides in me, and I in him. As the living Father sent me, and as I live because of the Father, so he who eats me will live because of me! (Jn 6:54-57)

11. Faith and Parousia

There is no noun in the Old Testament Hebrew vocabulary which corresponds exactly to "faith" or "belief." There is a verb, however, which underlies the general Old Testament notion of believing. The verb 'aman (from which Amen is derived, a call to belief which frequently precedes Jesus' solemn statements in John's Gospel) actually means "to be firm, solid, secure," and in the verbal form where it is usually translated into English as "to believe," it really means "to put one's firmness or security in another." Some exegetes have pointed out that the firmness or security is put precisely in another person, and is put in things only insofar as a person stands behind them.

John's vocabulary is not unlike that of the Old Testament. Whereas the noun "faith/belief " (Greek pistis) is very common in the rest of the New Testament, it never occurs in John's Gospel, and can be found only once in his letters. Instead, he uses the verb "to believe" (Greek pisteuein), implying that for him, as in the Old Testament, faith is more something one does, rather than something one has: faith is putting your ultimate security in another.

John frequently uses this verb in a peculiar and rather jarring manner. Instead of saying that someone "believes someone or something," or that he "believes in someone," John says a person "believes into." This unusual expression emphasizes the ongoing dynamism and interpersonal nature of believing, and also seems to stress the "becoming" aspect of faith. With only one exception, the object of "believing *into*" is Jesus (or Jesus' *name*—an equivalent Semitic idiom), or the Father through Jesus: "He who believes in[to] me believes not in[to] me, but in[to] him who sent me." (Jn 12:44b)

Jesus emphasizes, as we discussed earlier under *truth*, that to believe in him involves "knowing" or experiencing him as embodying the reality of the Father and committing oneself to him as such. He frequently determines the faith he demands from his disciples as faith in him that he is the one sent by the Father, in fact, that he is the very reality of God made visible and accessible to them. Since Jesus and the Father are one, the ultimate confession of faith in Jesus is that of Thomas after the resurrection, "My Lord and my God!" (Jn 20:28)

For John, then, faith involves a dynamic relationship to a person. When Jesus prefaces his statements with "Amen, Amen!" this is a call to say Yes to him and through him to the Father, much more than a Yes to a statement or a creed. To believe in[to] Jesus is to obey him, to come to him, to come to *know* him, that is, to enter into an interpersonal dynamic with him. In some ways the disciple's faith in Jesus and the love of God for him which he makes his own constitute the same reality:

Whoever confesses that Jesus is the Son of God, God dwells in him and he dwells in God. Thus we know and believe the love God has for us. God is love, and whoever abides in love abides in God, and God abides in him. (1 Jn 4:15-16)

To believe is to have the *word* within oneself. This implies an aspect of the communication of a reality

from the Father through Jesus in the Spirit to the believing disciple, as we explained in regard to the paschal
event. In his First Letter John says: "The testimony of
God is that he has borne witness to his Son. Whoever
believes in[to] the Son of God has this testimony within
himself." (1 Jn 5:9b-10a) This means that the believer
can himself become the fulcrum of belief in Christ for
others, just as the woman at the well was for her fellow
Samaritans. Here again recall how in the introduction
to his First Letter John calls others into a communion
of love with his fellowship, since his fellowship is with
Jesus and the Father. In the Christian community there
is the same access to Jesus as there was for the disciples
before the resurrection. "Blessed are those who have
not seen and have believed!" (Jn 20:29)

This was Jesus' prayer at the Last Supper: "I do not
pray for these only, but also for those who believe in[to]
me because of their word." (Jn 17:20) This same
thought occurs in Jesus' metaphor of the vine and the
branches. The disciples are already pruned and ready to
bear fruit because of the word.

The effect John most consistently associates with believing is that the believer has eternal life—he comes
from death to life; he comes out of the darkness into
light; he, though he die, will live and be raised up on the
last day. The believer enters into a whole new dimension of life, and therefore is said to be born anew of
God, becoming his child. He will not enter into judgment, he will not hunger or thirst, and he will experience Jesus as the Holy One of God. Because by his
belief the believer has entered into the life of God which
is love, he will receive the Holy Spirit, behold the glory
of God, and do the works that Jesus did, yes even
greater works. Jesus, who fervently prays for unity
amongst the believers, promises them that as believers

in him they will become a community, "sons of light" (Jn 12:36), a term we know from Qumran to designate a fellowship.

Faith in Jesus, a placing in him of one's security outside of himself, is, like love, strongly future-oriented. It is faith *into* Jesus. It means leaping beyond the confines of time and place and affirming that "the future will be for me, in and because of Jesus." In this sense faith sees not only one's past as integral to his history, but also what is to come. Although the stimulus of faith is Jesus as Alpha, faith looks toward Jesus as Omega, the Lord who by his coming will complete and fulfill our history. Since faith respects the future and places our firmness in him who is to come, faith, again like love, is an emptying out, the grain of wheat which by dying brings life abundantly.

Faith, just as love, demands that we embrace our human history and vibrate to its inner possibilities, both now and prospectively, not try to sidestep or bracket it. If our faith leads us to disdain the human situation and to seek the Lord apart from it, this is more a subtle form of despair than faith. Jesus, the Word who became incarnate in our history, awaits us at the end of and through our human future, not apart from it.

This future-oriented dimension of faith (which would seem to correspond in part to what Paul calls *hope*) is stressed in Jesus' Last Supper discourse. The disciples are troubled with the thought that Jesus is about to depart from them, and their future seems uncertain. Jesus tells them:

Do not let your hearts be troubled. You believe in[to] God, believe also in[to] me. There are many dwelling places in my Father's home. Why else would I have told you that I was going to prepare a place for you? I am indeed going to prepare a place for you, and I will

come again and take you with me, so that where I am
you may also be. And you know the way where I am
going. . . . I will not abandon you as orphans. I will
come back to you. (Jn 14:1-4, 18)

As we see so often in the Last Supper discourse, John
refers to the consummation of history, when the Father
will bring the unfolding of his word in the universe to
its completion in Jesus, as Jesus' *coming*. At that time
God's glory will through Christ be definitively revealed
into the world he has loved and it will become the New
Jerusalem, a new heaven and a new earth. "Although
we do not yet know what we shall be, we know that
when he appears we shall be like him, for we shall see
him as he is."

Then I saw a new heaven and a new earth, because the
former heaven and the former earth has passed away,
and the sea was no more. And I saw the New Jerusalem, the holy city, coming down from heaven from
God, prepared as a beautiful bride to meet her husband. I heard a great voice from the throne cry out,
"Now is the dwelling of God with men. He shall dwell
with them, and they shall be his people and he shall be
their God who is always with them. He shall wipe every
tear from their eyes, and there shall be no more death
nor mourning, no more crying out nor pain, because
the former world has passed away. . . . See, I am making everything new! . . . It is done! I am the Alpha and
the Omega, the Beginning and the End. To anyone who
thirsts I will give to drink without cost from the fountain of the water of life. Who wins the victory shall
have this heritage. I will be his God and he will be my
son." (Apoc 21:1-7)

"Behold, I am coming soon. I am the Alpha and the
Omega, the Beginning and the End."
Amen! Maranatha! Come, Lord Jesus!